A CHARTWELL-BRATT S

CW00781036

Computer Systems
Where Hardware Meets Software

Colin Machin

Department of Computer Studies
Loughborough University of Technology

Chartwell-Bratt   Studentlitteratur

© Colin Machin and Chartwell-Bratt 1988.

Chartwell-Bratt (Publishing and Training) Ltd
ISBN 0-86238-075-8

Printed in Sweden
Studentlitteratur, Lund

ISBN 91-44-23071-0   1 2 3 4 5 6 7 8 9 10 │ 1991 90 89 88

Preface

The interface between the hardware and system software in any computer system represents, arguably, the most important area of computer system design. It is here where the performance of the system can be influenced for better or for worse. The whole question of the interaction between these two elements is one that has taxed academics and designers alike for a number of years and still it is not clear that solutions have been found to all areas of consideration. One of the problems that creates this situation is of there being a limited number of people who are sufficiently skilled in *both* hardware and system software techniques to fully appreciate the impact of a decision in one design area upon the other.

It is with a view to producing graduates with skill in both design areas that the course partly represented by the present text was created. As a whole, the course provides the student with considerable insight into hardware design techniques in one half and provides an extensive course in operating systems in the second half.

This text mainly covers the hardware design aspect but is always mindful of the software implications of the design decisions that are made. Indeed, the final chapter deals with the way in which the hardware designer is able to assist the operating system writer. As such, this chapter forms a basic introduction to operating systems that all graduates of any computing discipline should have. The material deliberately avoids complex hardware components and systems that would otherwise mask the basic operation that is to be described.

As well as providing course material for undergraduates in computer science, its completeness and extensive index allow this text to be used as a reference book in industry.

Contents

Chapter 4 Memory Interfacing

Chapter 5 Peripheral Interfacing

Chapter 6 Input/Output Programming

Chapter 7 Interrupt Structures

Chapter 8 Direct Memory Access

Chapter 9 Introduction to Operating Systems

Appendices

List of Figures

Chapter 1

Basic Concepts

1.1 The Basic Computer System

The characteristic that separates an electronic computer system from a simple calculator is that the computer system acts upon a predefined sequence of instructions or *program*. This program is stored somewhere within the computer system and we are quite at liberty to change it by some means or another. When this type of computer first came into existence, it was referred to as a *stored program computer* in order to distinguish it from the previous type of computer that was designed and built for a *specific* task. The latter type could never be persuaded to perform any other task without it having to be physically modified in some way. We might refer to the computer, the exterior of which we are familiar with and the operation of which we are going to study, as a *general purpose computer.*

Any computer system is made up of a number of units or sub-systems each with their own well defined function. Almost regardless of the size of the computer system, all have a number of common units or sub-systems. These units or sub-systems make up the basic computer system around which other units or sub-systems may be placed in order to enhance the performance of the system in some way. There are five units or sub-systems in the basic computer system. These are shown in figure 1.1.

The *Central Processing Unit* (CPU or processor) is where the instructions that make up the program are executed. The CPU carries out all of the arithmetic and logical operations necessary to execute the program. It is also capable of making simple binary decisions (one way or the other) based upon the results of its calculations. A separate function of the CPU is that of control of much of the operation of the remainder of the system. Precisely how much control over the other parts of the system rests with the CPU depends upon the architecture of the system in question. In relatively simple systems, the CPU will have much more direct control over the running of the system than in a relatively more complex one. In the latter case, the responsibility for the overall running of the system will be devolved to other units, probably outside the CPU.

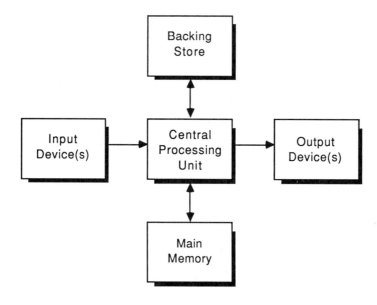

Figure 1.1 The *Five-Box* Model of a Computer System

This is much the same as the way in which a company may be run. If the company is small, one person might have direct, overall responsibility for *all* aspects of the running of that company. In a larger company a heirarchy of management will exist as no one person would be capable of handling the day to day running of everything. The CPU is itself made up of a number of sub-units all of which contribute to the performance of the processor or the system as a whole. We will learn more about the structure and operation of the CPU later.

The *Main Memory* is where the program that is to be executed by the CPU is stored along with the data upon which the program is working. There are a number of different types of main memory in use and it is in this area where we see some striking differences between computer systems put to different uses. The two basic types of main memory are *Read-Only Memory* (ROM) and *Random Access Memory* (RAM). As the name read-only suggests, this type of memory is designed to only allow its contents to be read. Its contents cannot usually be altered during the normal running of the computer system. In most cases, the contents of the ROM are placed into it before the ROM is attached to the system and is used to store some fixed program that the system will *always* run. Random access memory, on the other hand, allows data to be stored and later retrieved - it is read/write memory. Often, the contents of the random access memory are lost when the power to it is removed. We say that this type of memory is *volatile.* We will learn more about the different types of memory later, but it is worth saying at this point why different applications are likely to have different memory configurations. A small computer system, probably based around a microprocessor, used for some control application (such as the fuel injection system in a car) will be required to always do the same thing (control the fuel injection). The program to perform this task will be held, along with any constants relating to the system, in some form of read-only memory. In addition, a small amount of random access memory will have to be provided to store any variables that the control program uses. Thus a control application is likely to have much more read-only memory than random access memory. A large, general purpose computer, on the other hand, will have to be equipped with a large amount of random access memory to store both programs and data presented to it as the system runs. We cannot predict beforehand and preload into a read-only memory the programs that the system will have to run. It is likely, for a reason that will become clear later, that this type of computer system will have *some* read-only memory. It will, though, have a predominance of random access memory. Regardless of the type of memory that a system has, it is all accessed (read and written to) by means of a common scheme. The memory is divided up into storage units - each unit capable of storing a certain amount of information. Each of these units has a unique identifier associated with it. We call this identifier the *address.* The address is actually a number, with each successive storage unit (or location) having the next number in sequence. We will discover later the principle behind how the memory is split into these storage units.

If we build a system that has simply a CPU and some memory, we can execute programs with data. In order for that to be of any use, we must have some way of seeing the result of the execution of the program. For example, we could build a computer system that is capable of adding together two numbers, say 4 and 5. It will, hopefully, come up with the result 9. Unless this result can be conveyed to us in some way, the system is useless. Some form of *Output Device*, such as a printer, visual display screen or simple numeric only (calculator-type) display, is used to allow the system to convey the results of its labours to us. So, we now have a way in which the computer system that we have constructed can tell us what it has been doing. It can tell us that 4+5 is 9. That having happened though, the computer system has outlived its useful life. It can *only* go on telling us that 4+5 is 9 unless we can find some way of supplying two variables or *operands* upon which our system may perform its task of addition. We use some form of *Input Device*, such as a typewriter-style keyboard or simple numeric keypad, to pass information to the computer system. Once we have done this, we can make our system add together two numbers, call them x and y, which we supply by means of the input device and respond with the result through the output device. We have thus produced a general purpose number adding system - but nothing more than that. This looks very much like the control system that was mentioned earlier that *always* performs the same operations - but upon varying data. In appropriate circumstances, this is fine but it is no good if we wish to build a general purpose computer.

In order to build a general purpose computer, we need to find some way of providing not only the data but also the program that is to guide the computer. We could pass the program to the computer system through one of the input devices, but in most cases programs are large and input devices are relatively slow and the amount of time that it takes to load the program becomes too great. It is much more common, in general purpose computer systems other than perhaps the smallest, to store programs upon some form of *Backing Store*. This has the characteristic of being able to store quite large amounts of information in an easily accessable manner, where the time to load information to or from the backing store device is short. In other words, backing store usually provides for fast, large volume storage of information. As well as programs, the backing store may be used to store data such as the accounts of a television rental company. Most backing store devices are based upon some form of magnetic medium (tape, disk, etc.) and are therefore normally read/write devices. Some backing store devices are, however, read-only. A relatively old idea has recently come into use, namely of using optical disc technology (similar to domestic, laser read digital video or audio compact discs) to store vast amounts of read-only data.

Before we can go on to look in detail at the individual units of the computer system, we need to consider how information is represented and manipulated within the system and how we go about constructing the hardware to achieve this.

1.2   Information Representation

Within a computer system, information is represented and stored in the same way regardless of its type. Numbers are represented in the same way as text and this is represented in the same way as program instructions and so on. If we were to look at random within the computer memory at one item of information, we would be unable to tell what it represents. We would not know whether it is a program instruction, a number or anything else. It is only when the content of a particular area of memory is accessed that we know what it represents. If the central processor accesses a particular item of information at the time at which it is seeking a program instruction, then we must assume that it represents an instruction. If, instead, the central processor accesses an item whilst it is executing an instruction to add two numbers together, we must assume that it is an operand to the add instruction. It should be noted that there is no guarantee that *our* assumptions are correct. A fault in a program can easily lead to an item of data being collected by the central processor in all good faith as a program instruction and vice versa! Only certain processor have mechanisms (electronic ones!) for guarding against or at least trapping this type of error. To return to the main thread of our discussion, we need to consider how this information is stored within the memory and the processor.

One of the simplest of electronic devices is a switch. A simple on/off switch can be in one of two positions - closed or open (on or off) - and in each of these position will conduct or will not conduct (respectively) current. We can see this if we connect our switch to a lamp as shown in figure 1.2. When the switch is closed, current flows and the lamp will light. When the switch is open, current does not flow and the lamp extinguishes.

With more complex electronic devices, such as transistors, we find that this two state or binary operation is simple to achieve. We can easily configure a transistor in a circuit such that it may exist in one of two states. These happen also to be classed as on and off. We seek therefore an information representation scheme that can utilise this two state operation of the electronics from which our computer system is to be built.

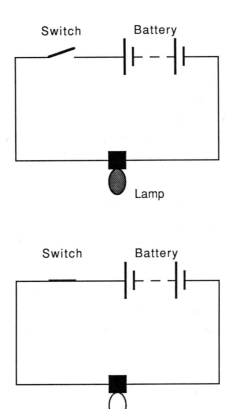

Figure 1.2 The On/Off switch and its use to light a lamp

We have already seen the word that describes the representation that is generally chosen - the *binary* system. We will now go on to look at how we can use the binary system to represent numbers.

1.2.1   The Binary System

Humans count in the decimal (or more strictly named denary) system. In this, numbers are represented with a *base* of *ten*. That is, the digits that go to make up a number are taken from the *ten* possible digits in the range {0 -> 9} and when more than one digit is used in a string, each successive digit position to the left representing the next successive power of *ten*, with the least significant digit representing 10^0 (or 1 as we normally know it). Thus the decimal number that we would write as 42081 actually represents (reading from the least significant digit):

$$
\begin{array}{llllr}
1 \text{ times } 10^0 = 1 \text{ times} & 1 & = & 1 \\
8 \text{ times } 10^1 = 8 \text{ times} & 10 & = & 80 \\
0 \text{ times } 10^2 = 6 \text{ times} & 100 & = & 0 \\
2 \text{ times } 10^3 = 2 \text{ times} & 1000 & = & 2000 \\
4 \text{ times } 10^4 = 4 \text{ times} & 10000 & = & 40000 \\
\hline
 & & & 42081 \\
\end{array}
$$

The binary system works in exactly the same way as the decimal system in that each successive digit taken from the range {0 -> number base - 1} represents the next successive power of the number base. However, the binary system differs from the decimal system in that the number base is *two* and not ten. Thus in the binary system each successive digit taken from the range {0 -> 1} represents the next successive power of 2. Thus the binary number 11101001 actually represents (reading from the least significant digit):

$$
\begin{array}{llllr}
1 \text{ times } 2^0 = 1 \text{ times} & 1 & = & 1 \\
0 \text{ times } 2^1 = 0 \text{ times} & 2 & = & 0 \\
0 \text{ times } 2^2 = 0 \text{ times} & 4 & = & 0 \\
1 \text{ times } 2^3 = 1 \text{ times} & 8 & = & 8 \\
0 \text{ times } 2^4 = 0 \text{ times} & 16 & = & 0 \\
1 \text{ times } 2^5 = 1 \text{ times} & 32 & = & 32 \\
1 \text{ times } 2^6 = 1 \text{ times} & 64 & = & 64 \\
1 \text{ times } 2^7 = 1 \text{ times} & 128 & = & 128 \\
\hline
 & & & 233 \\
\end{array}
$$

We call a binary digit a *bit* (a name perhaps derived from **bi**nary dig**it**). The number which we have been considering consists of eight binary digits, thus it is an 8-bit number. The maximum number that we can store in 8 bits is 255 (decimal). This number is 2^8 - 1 and in general the maximum that an n-bit binary number can store is 2^n - 1. Compare this with decimal, where, for example, the maximum value of a 3-digit number is 999. This is 10^3 - 1. In general, in any number base (b), the maximum value of an n-digit number is b^n - 1.

It is all very well being able to represent numbers in the binary system for the benefit of the electronics, but we must also be able to manipulate the information thus stored. Most importantly, we need to be able to perform arithmetic operations upon numbers stored in this way. Let us see, first, how we add two decimal numbers. Consider the addition of the two numbers 473 and 265. Remembering that each successive digit represents a successive power of 10, we start be adding the least significant digits of the two numbers. We add 3 to 5 to produce the answer 8. This we write down as the least significant digit of our result:

$$
\begin{array}{r}
473 \\
265 \\
\hline
8
\end{array}
$$

We then move on to the next pair of digits representing the multipliers of 10^2 and add these. From adding the two digits 7 and 6, we get the result 13. We cannot write this in a single digit position. Instead, we note that this represents 3 times the current power of 10 plus 1 times the next highest power of 10. Thus we write the least significant digit of this result (namely 3) and *carry* the surplus 10 as a 1 into the next digit position:

$$
\begin{array}{r}
473 \\
265 \\
\hline
38
\end{array}
$$
carry **1**

Upon considering the next digit position, we add the 4 and the 2 to the 1 carried from the previous power of 10, giving a result of 7. This we write as our most significant digit of the result:

$$
\begin{array}{r}
473 \\
265 \\
\hline
738 \\
\hline
\end{array}
$$

Thus our complete result is 738.

Let us now apply the same logic to the binary system. Let us add together 10010110 and 01011101. As with the decimal addition, we start by adding together the least significant digits of the two numbers. In this case it is 0 and 1, giving a result of 1:

$$10010110$$
$$01011101$$
———————
$$1$$

We then move on to the next digit position and add 1 to 0 again giving the result 1:

$$10010110$$
$$01011101$$
———————
$$11$$

In the next digit position we add 1 to 1. This appears to give us a result of 2. But, 2 is not permitted in this number base. In fact 1 + 1 in binary gives a result of 10. As in our decimal example, this represents 0 times the current power of 2 plus 1 times the next highest power of 2. As before, then, we *carry* the 1 into the next most significant digit position:

$$10010110$$
$$01011101$$
———————
$$011$$
carry **1**

The next digit position finds us adding together the 0 and 1 from this digit position to the carry from the previous one. This again gives us a result of 0 carry 1:

$$10010110$$
$$01011101$$
———————
$$0011$$
carry **1**

Now we add, in the next digit position 1 and 1 together with the 1 carried from the previous digit position. This seems to give us 3, but as with the 2 earlier, this is not within the binary system. We actually get 11, the least significant 1 belonging to this digit position and the most significant 1 belonging to the one *above* this:

$$
\begin{array}{r}
10010110 \\
01011101 \\
\hline
10011 \\
\end{array}
$$

carry **1**

Completing the addition presents no further problems and we end up with the result 11110011.

$$
\begin{array}{r}
10010110 \\
01011101 \\
\hline
11110011 \\
\hline
\end{array}
$$

As a double check and as an exercise in binary to decimal and decimal to binary conversion, we can check our binary addition in decimal. The binary nuumber 10010110 represents the decimal number 150 whilst 01011101 represents 93. Adding these together we get 243 which is indeed 11110011 in binary.

Before we leave binary addition, consider what happens when we add 150 to 150.

$$
\begin{array}{r}
10010110 \\
10010110 \\
\hline
\end{array}
$$

carry 1 00101100

We only get the expected result of 300 if we consider *9* bits as the addition of the most significant bits produced a carry beyond our 8 bits. Of course, we cannot store the result 300 in 8 bits and hence we see the result 44. The fact that a carry occurred out of the most significant bit is the signal to the fact that the result is incorrect. Many CPUs will *remember* any carry out of the most bit of the result in addition to possibly using it as an error signal. The use of this *carry flag* or *carry bit* might allow us to retrieve the potential error situation if further arithmetic operations are to be performed. In this case, we effectively have 9-bit working.

Subtraction of binary numbers follows the same rules that hold for the subtraction of decimal numbers in that if we find ourselves unable to subtract the two digits representing a particular power of the number base concerned, we *borrow* 1 from the next successive power and perform the subtraction from this newly formed number.

The 1 must be *paid back* when we reach the next digit position. As an example, we will work the above addition backwards by subtracting 01011101 from 11110011. The two least significant digit positions present no problem. Taking 1 away from 1 gives us 0 in the least significant digit position followed by taking 0 from 1 in the next to give 1:

$$11110011$$
$$01011101$$

10

In the third digit position, we need to subtract 1 from 0. This we cannot do and so we *borrow* a 1 from the next digit position giving now the opportunity to subtract 1 from 10 (2 in decimal). This gives us 1 in this digit position. Paying back the 1 that we borrowed from the fourth digit position is done, when we move on to that digit position, by adding 1 to the digit present in this position in the second number. Thus we now have to take 10 from 0. Applying our borrowing principle again gives us a 0 for the fourth digit:

$$11110011$$
$$01011101$$

0110

Remembering to pay back to the fifth digit and proceeding in the same fashion, we complete the subtraction and get the final result of 10010110 as we expected:

$$11110011$$
$$01011101$$

$$10010110$$

So far we have dealt only with positive numbers. A computer that is restricted to working only with positive numbers is likely to be of limited use. We now investigate how to represent and manipulate negative numbers.

1.2.1.1 Negative Numbers

In decimal representation, we use a special symbol, namely the minus sign (-), to indicate that a number is negative. We then take this into account in a special way when we are manipulating the numbers. It is quite feasible to develop a scheme similar to this for binary. Since a number is *either* positive or negative, we could use a single bit, with its ability to encode one of two states, to represent the sign of a number. This representation is known as *sign and magnitude* representation. Its use is uncommon since we unfortunately have to do what we do in decimal arithmetic and treat positive and negative numbers differently. It also gives us two representations of zero, namely +0 and -0! Because of this and because we can see how it would work (if used) from our knowledge of decimal arithmetic, no more attention will be given to this scheme here. It would be better if we could, within the computer, seek a scheme for representing negative numbers that does not require a separate, special action for their manipulation. We will investigate this possibility by seeing what happens when we *create* a negative number by subtracting a larger number from a smaller one. To start with, let us try subtracting 1 from 0 and thus see how -1 might be represented. For convenience, we will work in 8-bit binary notation.

$$
\begin{array}{ll}
00000000 & 0 \\
00000001 & 1 \\
\hline
11111111 & -1 \\
\hline
\end{array}
$$

We see that the borrowing principle that we considered earlier has led to a string of 1s in the result. If we performed the same operation upon 16-bit numbers, we would find that we ended up with sixteen 1s instead of eight and so on. So, we might suggest that -1 is represented by a string of, in our case, eight 1s. Let us see whether this is reasonable by attempting to add 2 back to the -1 and inspect the result.

$$
\begin{array}{ll}
11111111 & -1 \\
+\ 00000010 & +\ 2 \\
\hline
00000001 & 1 \\
\hline
\end{array}
$$

The result of adding 2 to -1 is, as we would expect, +1. So, it would appear that we can at least represent -1! Perhaps we should find out how to represent -2 by attempting to subtract 2 from 0.

$$
\begin{array}{ll}
00000000 & 0 \\
-\ 00000010 & -\ 2 \\
\hline
11111110 & -2 \\
\hline
\end{array}
$$

It would appear that -2 could be represented by 11111110. Again, in 16-bit representation, all bit positions above the least significant would contain a 1. You might like to confim that -2 is 11111110 in 8-bit representation by adding back 3 to see if this achieves +1. The reader may be assured that this will in fact be the case.

It will be noted, if this scheme of deriving negative numbers by subtraction from 0 is persued, that in all cases, a negative number will have a 1 in its most significant bit position. This is, in many ways, equivalent to our minus sign in decimal representation. In fact, we call the most significant bit of a number the *sign bit*. The sign bit differs from the minus sign of decimal representation in the fact that we do not need to change the rules of our arithmetic operations just because it is there. We have seen, albeit in passing, how we can add negative numbers without changing our arithmetic rules. As a further exercise, we may confirm the subtraction works satisfactorily with our newly derived representation by attempting two subtractions each yeilding a different type of result. Firstly we will subtract 2 from -1 to yield, hopefully, a further negative result (-3). Then we will subtract -2 from -1 to give a positive result (1).

$$
\begin{array}{rr}
11111111 & -1 \\
-\ 00000010 & -\ 2 \\
\hline
11111101 & -\ 3 \\
\end{array}
$$

$$
\begin{array}{rr}
11111111 & -1 \\
-\ 11111110 & -\ -2 \\
\hline
00000001 & 1 \\
\end{array}
$$

The binary representation that we have derived that allows us to use the same arithmetic procedures on positive and negative numbers is known as *2's complement* representation. We have formed the 2's complement of our example numbers by subtracting them from zero. This works for both positive and negative starting numbers. This however is a little tedious and it might be appropriate here to consider an alternative way of forming the 2's complement. The first step is to form the 1's complement. This is the simple, logic complement and is formed by simply inverting (0 becomes 1, 1 becomes 0) each and every bit in the number. The 2's complement is then formed from the 1's complement by adding 1. Let us, as a simple example, form the 2's complement of +1 in 8-bit representation.

$$00000001 \quad (+1)$$

$$
\begin{array}{ll}
11111110 & \text{(1's complement of 1)} \\
+\ 00000001 & \text{(plus 1 to form 2's complement)} \\
\hline
11111111 & \text{(-1, confirmed from above)} \\
\hline
\end{array}
$$

For the sake of completion and to prove that it works, we will produce the 2's complement of -1.

$$11111111 \quad (-1)$$

$$
\begin{array}{ll}
00000000 & \text{(1's complment of -1)} \\
+\ 00000001 & \text{(plus 1 to form 2's complement)} \\
\hline
00000001 & \text{(+1, QED)} \\
\hline
\end{array}
$$

The reader may wish to confirm that this scheme works for other numbers.

We might be forgiven for thinking that we have found a perfect representation for negative numbers. Indeed we have, but there are limitations upon the *use* of this representation. In particular, we must be careful with exactly how we interpret results. It was noted earlier that within an 8-bit binary pattern, we could represent numbers in the range 0 to 255 (decimal). However, we now learn that any number with the most significant bit set to a 1 is interpreted as negative. This is exactly half our possible numbers. Thus we can no longer represent numbers between 0 and 255. In fact, within 8 bits we can represent positive numbers in the range 0 (00000000 in 8-bit binary) to 127 (01111111) and negative numbers in the range -128 (10000000) to -1 (11111111). This brings us to the problem of interpretation of results. If we add 1 to 127, as follows:

$$
\begin{array}{ll}
00000001 & 1 \\
+\ 01111111 & +\ 127 \\
\hline
10000000 & 128 \\
\hline
\end{array}
$$

we get two different results depending upon whether we look at the binary result or the decimal one. The binary result 10000000 is, as we have just seen, -128. The decimal result is +128. There is something of a difference between these two but how do we

14

tell the difference? We note that we have already established that +128 (or any larger positive number) cannot be represented in 8-bit binary when negative numbers are in use. This makes matters even worse, since we have no idea that the result is *trying* to represent +128. It looks for all the world like -128. The key is in the fact that even though we were adding two positive numbers, the sign bit yielded a 1. This happened, in fact, because a carry occurred into the most significant bit of the result. We say, in this case, that *overflow* has occurred and that therefore the result should be treated as incorrect if negative numbers are in use. Of course, the CPU has no idea whether *we* are treating 10000000 as +128 or -128. We are at liberty to treat it as either since the arithmetic rules are the same whether we include negative numbers or not. Overflow is simply a means of denoting that the result should be disregarded if we are using negative numbers. As with a carry out of the most significant bit of a result, overflow may be used to signal an error condition and/or may be recorded in an *overflow flag* or *overflow bit*. Note that the overflow condition is, however, different from that recordered in the carry bit. Overflow is signalled upon a carry *into* the most significant bit of the result whilst carry is signalled upon a carry *out of* the most significant bit. Further, as we have already noted, overflow is of importance only when negative numbers are in use.

1.3 Logic Design

The choice of the binary system to represent information inside a computer system was based upon the ease with which electronic circuits can represent the two states *off* and *on*. The techiques of handling these states come under the heading of logic design. A complete treatment of logic design is outside the scope of this text, but it is necessary for the reader to have some understanding of the principles involved in order to appreciate later sections.

1.3.1 Logic Levels

The two states *'0'* and *'1'* are usually represented by voltage levels within the electronic circuits. For example, the popular TTL (transistor-transistor logic) scheme uses a voltage of less than 0.8V to represent a '0' and a voltage greater than 2.4V to represent a '1'. Any voltage between 0.8V and 2.4V is undefined but should not, in any case, occur. Under normal circumstances we disregard the actual *voltage* levels but instead concentrate upon the *logic* levels. An alternative to using '0' and '1' to describe our logic levels is to use the two terms *low* and *high*, respectively, with the abbreviations *L* and *H*.

1.3.2 Logic Variables

In any design, it is necessary to describe the operation of a particular block of logic in terms of its inputs and outputs. In order to do this, we usually assign names to the input and output *signals* and then construct an expression combining these names in the appropriate manner. The expressions utilise the same logic elements as the logic circuit that we eventually build. The reason for using an expression is to allow us firstly to clarify our ideas and secondly to apply certain tricks that may result in a simpler expression in much the sane way as we do in ordinary mathematics.

Sometimes, we need to express a logic variable in terms of a negative. For example, we may wish to include in a given expression some notion of the state of the weather and in particular whether or not it is raining. In binary logic terms, it is either raining or it is not raining. We could establish a logic variable R to represent the state *raining.* We could include this in a logic expression as the variable R such that if it is raining, R takes the logic value '1'. It might be convenient in some part of the expression to think in terms of the weather being *dry.* We could invent a new variable to represent this, namely D. Of course, if it is not raining, it is dry (at least in our definition above). It is wasteful to have two variables, *raining* and *dry*, when one would do. We have noted that *dry* is **not** *raining* and so we could express this condtion as such - *not raining*. We do this in logic expressions by placing a *bar* over the logic variable that we wish to treat in its opposite or *inverted* state. Thus

$$D = \overline{R}$$

in our example. In some logic circuits, the inputs are presented as their inverse. For example, we might wish to provide as an input to a circuit an indication this it is not raining. This would be done by introducing *only* the signal $\overline{R}$. More realistically, we shall see that in the Z-80 microprocessor, the signal that tells the processor to clean itself up ready to start executing program, namely *reset* is represented by a logic '0' or low level. This is usually written as $\overline{RESET}$. As this signal is active when low, it is known as an *active-low* signal.

In order to avoid confusion when we are describing systems that have both active-low and active-high signals mixed, we tend to avoid talking in absolute terms of '0' and '1' or low and high. Instead, we talk about a signal being *asserted* (active) or not. $\overline{RESET}$ is asserted when low in fact, although we do not completely express this. It is only when we wish to design a circuit to produce $\overline{RESET}$ that we need to actually know this it is active-low. This is particularly important in describing certain systems where the actual logic levels are disguised within the names of the signals. An example of this is the UNIBUS from Digital Equipment where most of the signals are active-low, but their names do not include the *bar*. We will be studying the UNIBUS and for the sake of consistency with the DEC literature and other texts, we will use the same signal names (without the *bar*) and talk of the signals being asserted. When a signal return to its opposite state, we talk of it as having been *removed*. Thus, when the Z-80 is to be released from its reset state, $\overline{RESET}$ is removed.

1.3.3 Logic Operators and Logic Expressions

The logic variable representing signals are to be combined in some way as represeneted by a logic expression. We now consider what sort of combination we can make between these variables. In normal communications one with another, we talk about combinations of conditions. The normal *operators* that we use to combine the logic variables in speech are *AND, OR* and *NOT*. Not surprisingly, these are the basic logic operators that we have available in the electronic representation.

As the AND operation behaves in logic much like the multiplication operator in arithmetic, we denote the AND operation as either '&' or '.'. Likewise, as the OR operation is similar in operation to addition, it is denoted as '+'. With these operators any logic system can be described by combining logic variables with these operators. For example, if the decision as to whether or not to go to the cinema is based upon the state of the weather and the attraction of the evening's television schedule, then we might express it as:

"I will go to the cinema if it is raining *and* there is nothing good on television".

It is trivial to turn this into a logic expression combining two variable - one concerning the weather and the other concerning the television schedules - with the AND operator between them.

Once we have an expression describing the operations that we require to perform, there are a number of techniques that can be applied to reach a stage of having a circuit diagram. We could apply the rules of logic to our expression in order to simplify it. These are the rules of *Boolean Algebra*. Alternatively we could apply one of the procedural methods of simplification such as *Karnaugh Maps*. The reader is left to investigate these techniques from other texts if it is considered necessary.

1.3.4 Logic Elements

At some point, it will be necessary to express the logic system in diagramatic form so that it can be built using the available logic elements. There are standard symbols for the operations AND, OR and NOT. An *AND-gate* with two inputs is shown in figure 1.3 along with a 2-input *OR-gate* and the element that provides the NOT function - an *inverter*. In the case of these three elements, the function of the element is clear. This may not always be the case. In order to express the function of a particular element in an unambiguous manner, it is common to use a *truth-table*. This expresses the way in which the inputs are combined to form the outputs. As an example, the truth tables for the elements shown in figure 1.3 are given in figure 1.4. It is clear from (a) that for the AND-gate the output is '1' *only* when the two inputs are '1'. For the OR-gate (b), the output is high (to use the alternative notation for logic levels) when either or both of the inputs is high.

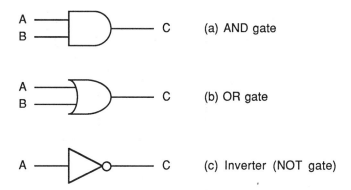

Figure 1.3 Symbols for the AND, OR and inverter logic elements.

A	B	C
0	0	0
0	1	0
1	0	0
1	1	1

A	B	C
0	0	0
0	1	1
1	0	1
1	1	1

A	C
0	1
1	0

(a) AND-gate   (b) NOR gate   (c) Inverter (NOT gate)

Figure 1.4 Truth-tables for the AND, OR and inverter logic elements.

There are two more commonly used logic elements that require attention. These are the *NAND-gate* and *NOR-gate*. The logic symbols and truth-tables for these elements are shown in 1.5. Quite simply, a NAND-gate performs precisely the same logic function as an AND-gate, but its output is inverted. The NOR-gate is similar in that it performs an OR-function but also produces an inverted output.

Not only for completeness, but also because they will be used later on in this text, are included two more logic elements. The *exclusive-OR-gate*, as can be seen from figure 1.6, produces a '1' output when either *but not both* of its inputs is a '1'. The *exclusive-NOR-gate* exhibits the same function but provides an inverted output.

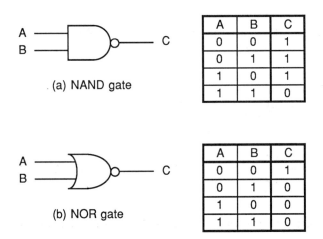

(a) NAND gate

A	B	C
0	0	1
0	1	1
1	0	1
1	1	0

(b) NOR gate

A	B	C
0	0	1
0	1	0
1	0	0
1	1	0

Figure 1.5 Symbols and truth-tables for NAND and NOR logic elements.

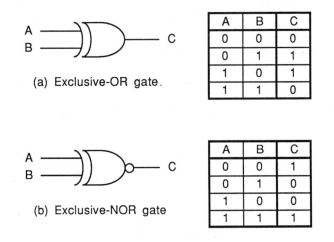

(a) Exclusive-OR gate.

A	B	C
0	0	0
0	1	1
1	0	1
1	1	0

(b) Exclusive-NOR gate

A	B	C
0	0	1
0	1	0
1	0	0
1	1	1

Figure 1.6 Symbols and truth-tables for Exclusive-OR and Exclusive-NOR logic elements.

It is worth noting that in the TTL series of gates already mentioned, the gates with inverted outputs are cheaper than those with true outputs.

All of the elements that have been introduced so far (except the inverter) have been shown as having two inputs. There are available larger versions of these gates, offering up to perhaps eight inputs. Commonly available packages include 2, 3, 4 and 8-input NAND gates and 2 and 3-input NOR gates. Wherever possible, we will attempt in later designs to use only these elemets

1.3.5 Negative Logic

It has been noted that in some situations, a signal may be presented as active-low. It would seem that there is a need to invert the signal thus presented before it can be used in a circuit. This is not the case. Applying DeMorgan's Law - one of the rules of logic, the detail of which does not concern us here - we find that the application of active-low inputs makes life easy rather than difficult. The practical result of DeMorgan's Law is that if we invert the inputs into a NOR-gate, we produce an AND-function. Similarly, if we invert the inputs into a NAND-gate, we produce an OR-function. Thus if we are provided with two active-low inputs that we need to AND together, we simply feed them to a NOR-gate.

Another piece of theory concerning logic systems, again the detail of which does not concern us here, says that *any* logic system may be built using *only* NAND or NOR gates. We generally do not bother to abide completely by this as it is often the case that elements exist to perform many of the sub-functions that we require. However, we do often try to restict ourselves to only NAND and NOR gates because this is likely to produce more cost-effective circuits.

1.3.6 Circuits with Memory

It is not only within the computer's memory itself that there is a need for remembering the state of one thing or another. For example, as the computer runs, it takes instructions from the memory (instruction fetch) and carries them out (instruction execution). It is reasonable to assume that it is necessary to keep track of whether the computer is fetching or executing. Thus one of two states needs to be remembered. This we can do with a simple on/off condition as we have seen before, but we need a element that can remember.

It is possible to construct this memory using two 2-input NOR gates. The so called NOR gate ring and is shown in figure 1.7. Assume that both inputs S and R are held low ('0') and that output Q is also low. The lower NOR gate has both inputs low. This gives a high output on P. The upper NOR gate has one input low and the other high. This gives us a low output. It can be seen that the system is stable in this state. The output of each NOR gate is holding the conditions for the output of the other gate. Now apply a high ('1') to the S input. The lower NOR gate now has one input high and the other low. This results in the output changing to a low. This is applied to the upper NOR gate together with the low still on the R input. The result is that the upper NOR gate now flips to a 1. This is fed to the lower NOR gate, but no change in the output occurs.

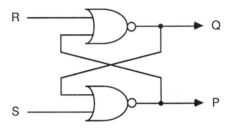

Figure 1.7 NOR-gate Ring

The system is again stable, but in the opposite sense. Now we see what heppens when the high on S is removed. The lower NOR gate still has one of its inputs high resulting in a low output on P. The condition on the upper NOR gate remian unchanged. Thus our circuit has *remembered* the application of the high on S even after is has been taken away. Now what happens if we apply 1 high to the R input? The output of the upper NOR gate flips to a low in response to having one of its input high. This is fed together with the still low S input to the lower NOR gate. The two lows on the lower NOR gate result in a high output. This combines with the high on R in the upper NOR gate to leave the Q output unchanged at low. When the high on R is removed, the output of the upper NOR gate remains low due to the fact that one of its inputs is still high. Thus our circuit has remembered the application of the high on R. It is perhaps clear that R and S were not chosen as arbitrary names for the inputs. We note that a high applied to S *sets* the output Q to high whilst a high on R clears or *resets* the output Q to low. Thus S and R are set and reset, respectively. Note also that whenever Q is low, P is high and *vice versa*. P is always the inverse of Q and so we re-label P as $\overline{Q}$. Since the state of the outputs is seen to flip from high to low and back again, the curcuit is known as a *set-reset flip-flop*. This is often abbreviated to SR (or sometimes RS) flip-flop. It is possible to configure two NAND gates in a NAND gate ring to achieve a similar result. The reader may wish to try this and note any differences.

As we have said, we do not always *build* the logic elements that we require from NAND or NOR gates even though this is possible. Often it is more convenient to use a ready-packaged version. This is true in the case of a flip-flop. The integrated circuit manufactureres have identified a need for flip-flops and therefore manufacture them for us. Internally they may utilise two NOR gate or whatever, but to the designer they simply become *black-box* devices that have a well-defined relationship between inputs and outputs. We would include these in circuit diagrams by drawing the appropriate circuit symbol such as that shown in figure 1.8 for an SR flip-flop. There are other types

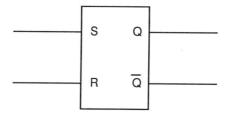

Figure 1.8 Symbol for Set/Reset Flip-Flop

of flip-flop available. One type, the *D-type flip-flop*, allows data presented at the D (data) input to be *latched* at the point in time at which a clock pulse is applied to the Ck (clock) input. The D input can take on any sequence of highs and lows without affecting the output. It is only *as* the Ck input goes from low to high (the *rising edge*) that the data is stored. The D-type flip-flop has two further inputs that allow it to be used rather like an SR flip-flop. The $\overline{PST}$ input is an active-low preset that sets Q high and $\overline{CLR}$ is an active-low clear that sets Q low. These two inputs override the D/Ck inputs such that if either $\overline{PST}$ or $\overline{CLR}$ are active, no data will be latched even if a rising edge occurs on the Ck input. The circuit symbol for a D-type flip-flop is shown in figure 1.9.

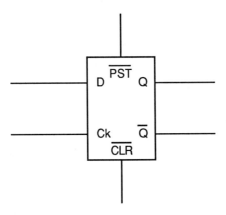

Figure 1.9 Symbol for D-type Flip-Flop

There are many other specialised devices covering a wide range of operations. We shall investigate them as they are required.

Chapter 2

Processor Architecture

2.1 The Centre of Action

The Central Processing Unit (CPU or simply *processor*) is at the heart of the computer system hardware. It is responsible for providing all of the arithmetic, logic and other operations required for the running of a program. Elements within the CPU may also be responsible for (at least some of) the control of the remainder of the system. In order to keep our ideas simple at this stage, we will consider a CPU that is purely responsible for executing the program. As our knowledge of the system develops we will see how many other tasks might become the responsibility of the CPU.

The CPU simply executes program instructions that are stored in the memory in strict order unless otherwise told by a special type of instruction that allows the processor to skip to another part of memory. The cycle of events is, quite obviously, that the processor goes to the memory at the position that stores the next instruction to be executed and reads it in. This is the instruction *fetch* operation or *sub-cycle*. It then examines the instruction to find out what it is to do - the *decode* sub-cycle. Having decided what it is to in order to carry out the operation requested, it goes ahead and does it. This is the *execution* sub-cycle. This cycle of *fetch-decode-execute* is carried out over and over again. In fact, it continues until either a special instruction that halts the operation of the processor is executed or until the power is removed.

In general terms, the processor consists of a number of sub-units each with their own job to perform. The main sub-unit of the CPU is the Arithmetic and Logic Unit (ALU). This is where the actual operations that are required to execute the program take place. Data is fed to the ALU from a number of places, but primarily from the memory where the constants and variables of the program are stored. However, it may be that some items of data are required often and it would be inefficient to continually take them from the memory and restore them again if changed. This is particularly the case when a sequence of instructions are being executed that perform some complex arithmetic operation. Instead, another sub-unit within the processor, will provide one or more temporary storage locations which are accessable to the program. These are the *general purpose registers* of the processor, often simply referred to as *the* registers. Access to the registers is usually much faster than to the memory as the registers form part of the processor rather than being outside it and so our efficiency requirement is met. We will see in greater detail later how the registers are accessed and used when we look at the way in which instructions are encoded.

Other registers exist within the procesor that have *special* uses assigned to them. For example, the processor needs to keep track of which instruction it is currently executing. It does this with a special register called the *program counter* (PC). Rather than pointing to the instruction currently being executed, it actually points to (contains the address of) the next instruction to be fetched from memory. Thus it is incremented after each instruction fetch from memory. It is possible that the program counter will be incremented by passing it through the ALU. We will encounter a number of other special purpose registers as we find out more about the operation of the processor. In most processors, the program is allowed access to some of the special purpose registers for certain operations whilst other registers are purely for the use of the processor in its various functions. An example of the latter is the *memory address register* into which the processor places the address of the memory location that it wishes to access. This may be utilised a number of times during the fetch and execution of a single instruction and is not, therefore, one of the registers to which the program has direct access.

2.2 The Arithmetic and Logic Unit

The Arithmetic and Logic Unit is basically a very simple device. It is capable of performing a limited number of operations on one or two binary patterns which we will call *operands*. The ALU may be implemented in discrete logic specially designed for the purpose or it may be based on a pre-packaged, integrated circuit ALU that is capable of doing at least some of the work required. The ALU can be visualised as having two inputs *A* and *B* upon which the operation defined by the *ALU function* inputs is performed to produce the output *C*. The ALU as seen *from the outside* is shown in figure 2.1.

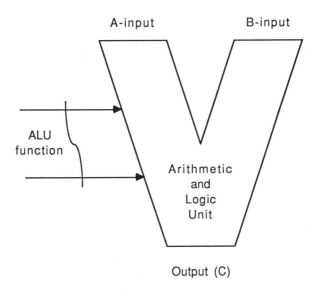

Figure 2.1 ALU - External View

Internally, the ALU might consist simply of number of blocks, each with a very specific job to perform and each controlled by one or more of the ALU function inputs. Figure 2.2 shows the elements that might make up a relatively simple ALU. At the heart of the ALU is a block that is capable of performing basic operations on two binary patterns. These operations will probably be limited to addition, possibly subtraction and the logical operations such as AND and OR. It is at this stage that we would probably make use of a pre-packaged ALU. In the standard 7400 TTL (transistor-transistor logic) series is the 74S381. This is a 4-bit ALU that can perform in a few nanoseconds ($1nS = 10^{-9}$ S) one of eight operations as defined by a 3-bit function select code as defined in figure 2.3. If we only need a 4-bit ALU, this integrated circuit is fine, but it is likely that we will need to provide a somewhat wider ALU. This can be achieved by placing any number of these ALUs *side-by-side* until we have achieved the desired number of bits. This poses a problem, though. The arithmetic operations are capable

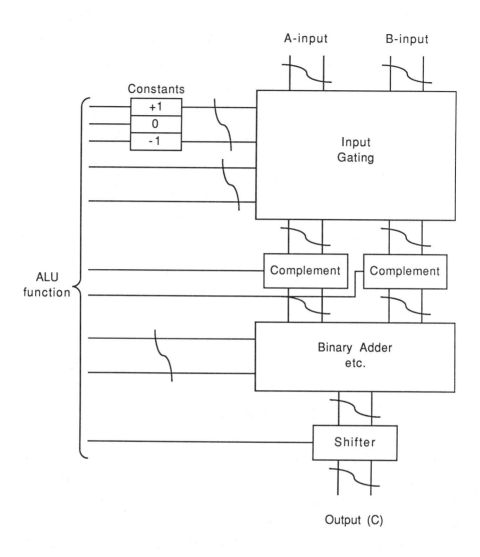

Figure 2.2 ALU - Internal Structure

of producing a carry (or borrow) from any particular bit. This is taken care of within the groups of four bits by the 74S381. However, when a carry occurs out of one group of four bits into the next, this must be noted and acted upon. Thus, we can see that the carry will *ripple* through the blocks of four bits and our operation time will therefore increase. It is possible to add some further logic (it comes in an integrated circuit, fortunately) that predicts the carry from one block of four to the next, thus saving a proportion of the time otherwise required. This is known as *carry look-ahead* and with the dedicated carry look-ahead generator, the 74S381 can be used to perform a 16-bit addition in 26nS and a 32-bit addition in only 34 nanoseconds (nS).

Function Select			Arithmetic/Logic Operation
S2	S1	S0	
0	0	0	Clear [C = 0000]
0	1	1	B MINUS A
0	0	0	A MINUS B
0	1	1	A PLUS B
1	0	0	A XOR B
1	1	1	A OR B
1	0	0	A AND B
1	1	1	PRESET [C = 1111]

Figure 2.3 74S381 ALU Function Table

Preceding this block, on each of its inputs, is likely to be a block that is capable of complementing (swapping 1s for 0s and *vice versa*) the inputs to the adder block. Preceding these there is likely to be the input gating. This is a block, built up from simple logic elements (gates), that can route into either complement block either the A-input or the B-input or one of a number of special constants that will be useful in the arithmetic and logic operations. These are likely to include +1, 0 and -1. The final block follows the main operation block and this is capable of shifting the output of the adder usually only one place to either the left or the right.

The information handled by the ALU will, as we have seen, come from one or more of the general purpose registers. The results generated by the ALU will probably be returned to one of the same set of registers. Thus the two inputs to the ALU and its output will be connected to the general purpose register block. This is usually done in such a way that *any* register may be fed to either ALU input and the ALU output may, likewise, be fed back to *any* register. This is achieved by placing the ALU and the registers on the register highway as shown in figure 2.4.

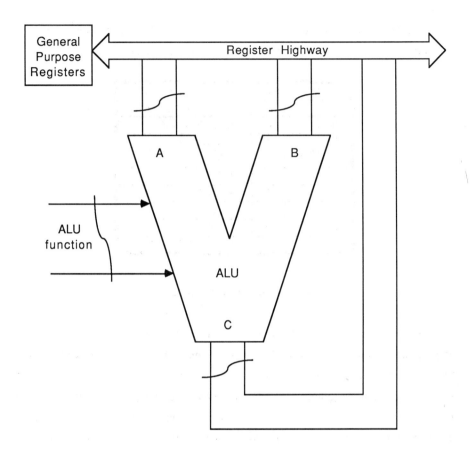

Figure 2.4 ALU connected to the general purpose register block via the Register Highway

In some processors, it may be possible to take the operands from the general purpose registers or from memory. Within the processor, the contents of a particular memory location may be assumed to be presented in an internal register known as the memory buffer register or memory data register. This must also have a path to the ALU. Thus we place the memory buffer register on a highway together with the general purpose register block. To reflect the fact that this highway is no longer exclusively for the use of the general purpose register block, we rename it the Internal Data Highway. The complete structure is shown in figure 2.5.

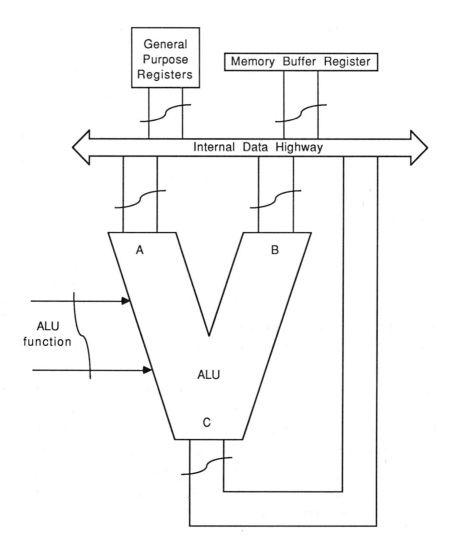

Figure 2.5 ALU access to both the General Purpose Registers and Memory

2.3 The Instruction Set

All CPUs are capable of adding numbers together, subtracting numbers from one another, performing logical operations (AND, OR etc.). Some processors (but by no means all) are capable of performing more complex operations such as multiplication and division! Such operations are known as *arithmetic and logic* operations. In addition, all CPUs are capable of making simple (one way or the other) decisions. These operations are known as *transfer of control* operations.

2.3.1 Arithmetic and Logic Operations

In order to understand how CPU instruction sets are derived, we will start by looking at the operation of addition. The first thing that we note is that we have to find some way of informing the CPU that we wish it to perform an addition operation. We do this by encoding the operation in some unique way. We call this encoded form of the operation that we wish to perform the *operation code* or op-code. For convenience, there is usually a *human* way of expressing this encoding. This is known as the op-code or instruction *mnemonic* as it is usually a short sequence of letters that in some way reflects the operation to which it relates. In the case of the addition operation, we could encode this in human terms as ADD. In fact, in the what follows, we will use these mnemonic representations as though they were the computer-based encodings. The next thing that we note is that the addition operation has three variables or *operands* associated with it. For convenience we will call these X, Y and Z, where the addition operation is defined as:

$$Z := X + Y.$$

Note the use of the symbol ":=". This is the assignment symbol and may be read as *takes the value* of or *becomes*. This symbol is used to distinguish it from "=" or *is equal to*, which is used to test the equality of two variables when making decisions. We see quite plainly that of these three operands, two (X and Y) are source operands and provide the data for the operation and one (Z) is the destination operand where the result of the addition will be placed.

We could conceive of an instruction format that allows us to specify, in addition to the instruction (ADD in this case), an indication of where each of the three operands are located. In this case we would write into the instruction the location at which the CPU will find the two source operands (X and Y) and the location at which we would like the result stored (Z). This we could write as:

ADD Z,Y,X

and rely upon the CPU to interpret this as "collect two operands from locations X and Y, add them together and place the result in location Z". We see here that we have written an instruction with three distinct operands. It is possible to construct a CPU instruction set that allows any instruction to have (up to) three operands. We call this, not surprisingly, a *three address machine*. The complete instruction encoding must include a space for the op-code and spaces for the three operands. This might appear in the computer's memory as:

op-code	dest	source 1	source 2
ADD	Z	X	Y

Of course, not all operations require three operands. The operation that negates a number (the unary minus operation) requires only two operands:

Y := -X

which we might encode as:

NEG Y,X

If this operation were defined on a three address machine, one of the three operand spaces within the instruction would be left blank. Only one source operand and the destination operand would need to be supplied. Although the human form of this instruction shows only two operands, the representation within the memory will still contain all three, although one of them (the second source operand) will be ignored. It is tempting to think that this operand space will be left *blank*, but it is unlikely that we could find a suitable encoding to mean *no operand present*. If we take the symbol "-" to mean *has no significance in this context*, then we could view the internal representation of this instruction as:

op-code	dest	source 1	source 2
NEG	Y	X	-

If all three operands are to be in memory, we must provide enough space in the instruction format to accomodate three memory addresses. This consumes a lot of space and is particularly inefficient when a given instruction does not have all three operands defined, but we wish, for one reason or another, to maintain the same format across all instructions. Many CPU instruction formats restrict the number of operand addresses that may be used for any instruction to two. These *two address machines* define their instructions to have one source operand address and one destination operand address. Whilst this is sufficient for our NEG instruction, it is, of course, insufficient for the ADD instruction. The way that the instruction is interpreted has to be redifined in this case by placing a slightly different meaning upon the operand addresses that appear in the instruction. For an operation that requires three operands (source1, source2 and destination) to be defined in a two address machine's instruction format, the destination operand address is used additionally as the address of one of the source operands. It usually doubles as source1 - the first source operand. The order of the operands is important in operations which are not commutitive, such as subtraction, although not in the case of our ADD example. Thus, we are restricted to operations such as:

ADD X,Y

which would be taken to mean:

X := X + Y

X being the shared first operand and destination. This might be encoded as:

op-code	dest/source 1	source 2
ADD	X	Y

It must be made clear that our ADD instructions still has three operands in reality - we saw them above:

$$X := X + Y.$$

It is only within the two-address instruction format that we insist that the instruction be coded with two operand *addresses*. This apparent reduction in flexibility within instructions turns out to be of little significance when we start to write programs as often these operations form only part of a much longer, more complex sequence.

We have made an assumption so far that the operands for a given instruction are in memory and that the operand addresses are given within the instruction. The CPU will need to be able to access data from the memory in order to perform upon it the operation defined by that instruction. If the programmer requires that a fairly complex calculation be carried out, he must split that calculation up into a number of smaller steps, each of which can be performed by a single CPU instruction. There are likely to be, in this case, a number of items of data that are required frequently during the sequence of instructions that make up the calculation. Some of these may be the variables within the calculation or may be intermediate results. Since it takes a certain amount of time for the processor to make access to the memory, it would seem sensible for the CPU to have somewhere close at hand in which to store frequently used data items or intermediate results for more rapid access. Most processors provide this local storage by having one or more general purpose *registers* within them. A typical processor might have eight or sixteen of such registers. As there are fewer registers within the processor than there are locations within the memory, the "address" of a register is going to be shorter than that of a memory location and will therefore take less space to define. If we define an instruction format in which one of the operands is a register, we are going to have a more economical representation. We could, for example, redefine out two address machine instruction format to use a register for the destination/source1 operand. This would mean that we would produce a shorter instruction, but at the expense of restricting one of the operands to being *only* a register address. We have already noted that this may not be as great a restriction as it seems. Thus we have a new type of instruction format - one that relates to what is called a *one-and-a-half address machine*. The "one" address is that of the second operand and relates to memory, the "half" address being that of the register that contains the first operand and, after execution of the instruction, the result.

Some early processors and some rather specialised processors of the present have only *one* register. This special register is called *the accumulator*. In any given instruction it may supply one of the operands and/or provide somehwere for the result to be placed. For example, for an addition operation, the processor would take operand1 from the accumulator and operand2 from memory. The result would then be placed into the accumulator. We only need to supply a single operand address within the instruction and thus this format is even more economical than the one-and-a half address machine. During complex calculations, we may have to continually move items of data to and from the accumulator. The penalty for instruction representation economy in the *one-address machine* is perhaps harder to live with in this case than in the case of the one-and-a-half address machine. If we wish to add the contents of memory location X to that of the accumulator, we simply write something like:

ADD X

which would be encoded as:

op-code	operand
ADD	X

Operations that naturally have only one operand, such as NEG, will normally take the operand from the accumulator and return the result back to the accumulator. Such an operation would be understood as "negate the contents of the accumulator".

Even more specialised types of processor have an instruction format that has (for the most part) no operands. The *zero address* machine sounds an impossiblity, but is easily explained by the fact that such machines use a structure called a *stack*. A stack is constructed in memory and is an area of otherwise unassigned memory within which we can store items of data on a temporary basis. A stack may be thought in much that same way as a pile of coins. We may add coins only to the top of the pile and when we wish to remove one, the only one which we can access (without disturbing the pile and risking confusion) is the one currently at the top. A stack is exactly the same in operation. We place items on to the top of the stack and take items from the top of the stack. When we place a coin on top of the pile, the others below it in the pile do not physically move down, but may be thought of as moving down logically. In just the same way, our stack in memory does not move, we simply assign memory to data items as they are stacked and then return it as free as we unstack items. The stack is organised around a pointer, called the *stack pointer* (SP). The stack pointer always contains the address in memory of the top item in the stack. When we wish to add an item to the stack, the stack pointer must first be updated to point to the next free location in the stack area. Then the data may be written to memory at the address given by the stack pointer. Unstacking an item is a straightforward matter of reading off the item at the address given by (we say *pointed to by*) the stack pointer and then updating the pointer to reflect the loss of an item. A stack may be constructed in the main, general purpose memory or it may be in special, reserved memory. It is likely that a zero-address machine will have its stack in memory set aside for the purpose. In either case, it is possible for the stack to *grow* in either direction. That is, the address held in the stack pointer will either reduce or increase as items are added to the stack. It is more common for the stack pointer to reduce - that is for the stack to *grow towards 0*. The stack pointer will probably never attain a value of zero, we simply use this expression to denote the direction of the stack. If we assume a stack which does grow towards 0, we can look at an example of stack manipulation. Suppose the stack pointer contains the address 1234. This tells us that the item currently on top of the stack is at location 1234. Let us assume that this is the number 54. If we now stack another item (the number 73, say), the stack pointer will move to point to location 1233 and the stack will look like:

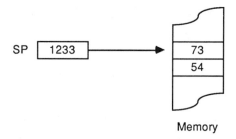

Memory

If we perform an operation to unstack an item, we get back the 73 that we last put on to the stack and the stack pointer reverts to pointing at the 54.

Having learnt about stacks, we can now see how this helps us to create a zero address machine. As long as we have at least two instructions that allow for stack manipulation, we can perform all other operations using the stack. We need an operation to copy an item from memory on to the stack and one to unstack an item and place it in memory. These PUSH and POP operations, respectively, are the only ones in the instruction set that require operand addresses. All other operations take any necessary parameter(s) from the stack and return any result to the stack. Thus, if we wished to add together the two numbers stored in memory locations X and Y, returning the result to memory location Z, we would firstly have to copy the contents of both locations X and Y to the stack, perform the addition and then return the result from the stack to memory location Z. This we could do with the sequence:

PUSH   Y

PUSH   X

ADD

POP   Z

Note that we PUSHed Y on to the stack first. This is so that the first operand (X) would be at the top of the stack when the ADD operation took place. This is important for non-commutative operations. It might appear that we have arrived at the ultimate in compactness of instruction representation - but at too great a cost in terms of programming effort. It has taken four instructions in this machine to perform an addition that required only one instruction in the three address machine. When we consider the operations required to perform a long calculation, we see that many of the intermediate results that are produced may be stored on the stack for later use. In fact, there exists a well documented technique for turning any arithmetic expression (or even assignment) into a form suitable for processing with a stack machine. This *Reverse Polish* form of an expression is simply a string of names of data items and operators. The expression is evaluated by pushing data items on to the stack in the order in which they occur in the string and applying the operators as they occur in the string. Many high-level computer language compilers and interpreters make use of this technique of organising arithmentic operation around a stack. Because of this, programs translated in this way from high-level languages can be run very efficiently on a stack machine.

2.3.2   Transfer of Control Operations

It has already been noted that CPUs offer programs the ability to make simple binary (one way or the other) decisions. This involves modifying the program counter, if some condition is met, to reflect a change in the flow of processing. We refer to this change of flow as *branching* or *jumping* and to the instructions involved as branch or jump instructions. Conditions that might be tested include whether or not the result of the previous arithmetic or logic operation is zero or less than zero or greater than zero, whether or not overflow occurred in the previous arithmetic operation and so on. We might refer to these operations as *jump on zero, jump on non-zero, jump on less than zero* and so on. Often a processor will summarise the result of an arithmetic or logic operation within a set of *flag* bits, usually collected together in the *flag register*. There will be one bit for each possible condition - zero, overflow, etc. The execution of a branch instruction is thus a matter of the processor examining one or more flags and modifying the program counter if the flag (or flag combination) is as specified for the given condition. The branch instruction must contain two pieces of information. It must give the condition upon which a branch is to be made and it must give the address to which transfer of control is to be made if the condition is met. The former is part of the encoding of the instruction whilst the latter may be no more than a fully specified memory address.

Not every transfer of control is necessarily *conditional*. There are many situations in which the program may wish to *always* jump to some location other than the one that follows naturally. We could contrive to force a zero result and then jump on zero, but this is unnecessary. We have a unique instruction code for this *unconditional transfer* operation.

2.4 Addressing Modes

Most processors provide a number of different ways of representing the address of one or more of the operands of a given instruction. For example, we have already seen that an instruction may contain the *actual* or *effective* operand address. This requires that the instruction format provides sufficient space to accomodate the address. This may be as few as 16 bits in a relatively small processor (giving a maximum addressing capability of 64K) or may be 24 or more bits in a larger processor. This addressing technique or *mode* is known as *direct* addressing since the address contained within the instruction is the *actual* address of the operand in question as in figure 2.6. As well as providing a means for specifying operand addresses within memory, this mode is also used in branch instructions. In this case, the address given is of the actual memory location to which the program is to transfer control if the condition is met.

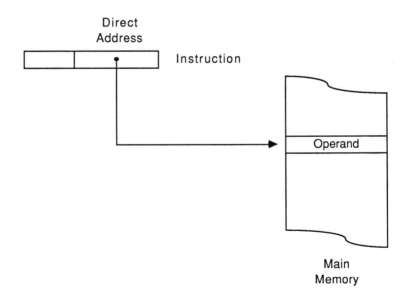

Figure 2.6 Direct Addressing

Often, the program that is running does not know the actual address at which data is stored. It may have to "calculate" the address when, for example, it is adding up a list of numbers. The program could modify itself to change the operand address within the instruction to that which it wishes to access, but this is undesirable. Instead, a further addressing mode is introduced that allows the instruction to specify where the *address* of the operand may be found. Usually, the address of the operand is stored within a register (in most cases one of the general-purpose registers) and it is the register identifier that is given within the stored instruction. This addressing mode is known as *indirect* addressing as the actual operand address is a level removed from the address given within the stored instruction. The diagram in figure 2.7 illustrates this. The

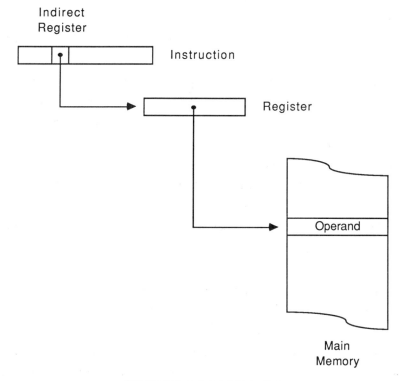

Figure 2.7 Indirect Addressing

indirect addressing mode is also used in branch instruction. Here, the processor is directed to branch to the address given the contents of the specified indirect source (normally a register as before).

It is sometimes necessary for a program to work systematically through a list of data items that can be thought of as somehow *belonging* together. The whole list might be known by some name and each element of the list as some offset or index from the start of the list. A single dimension array fits this description where the array as a whole is known by its name - *ARRAY*, for example - and each element is known by its index within the array - *ARRAY(3)* being the third element, for example. Many processors offer an addressing mode that matches this. It is known, for obvious reasons, as *indexed* addressing. The usual way in which indexed addressing is organised is that the base address (represented by the name *ARRAY* in our case) is given within the instruction whilst the index is provided in a register nominated by the instruction. The processor will add the number that it finds in the nominated register to the base address found within the instruction to form the actual or "effective" address. Thus, to access *ARRAY(3)*, we might place both the address of *ARRAY* and the identification of a register containing the number 3 within the instruction. Some processors will always increment the contents of the specified register to move on to the next data item, whilst others may be instructed to do so. In our case this would mean that *ARRAY(4)* would be accessed if the same instruction is executed again and so on. Figure 2.8 illustrates two different ways of perceiving indexed addressing. The first shows indexing in use in the array context that we have seen above, whilst the second shows the hardware in action with its adding operation. Indirect addressing is also sometimes used with transfer of control instructions. There is an implied indirection in this operation and when used with a branch instruction, control is transfered to the address given by the contents of the selected "array" location.

A specialised form of indexed addressing in which the register containing the index is the program counter gives rise to *relative*, sometimes called *PC-relative*, addressing. In this, the address of the operand is stored within the instruction as an offset from the instruction address. When the processor adds this relative address to the program counter, it ends up with the actual operand address. The effect of this is shown in figure 2.9. Relative addressing is also used for branch instructions. Here the jump address is stored as an offset from the current program counter position. If all memory accesses and transfers of control can be made with this form of addressing, the program may be moved to any position within the memory and still run satisfactorily. Such a program is said to be made up of *position independent code*.

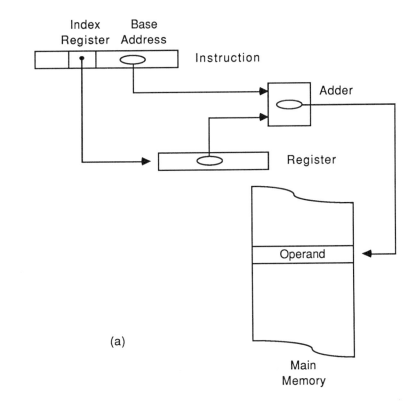

(a)

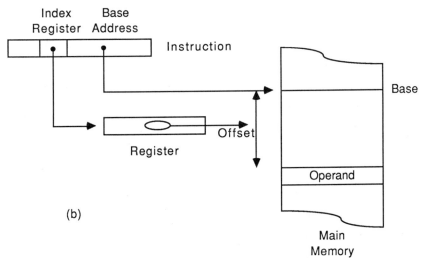

(b)

Figure 2.8 Indexed Addressing

The four addressing modes direct, indirect, indexed and relative form the basis of the majority of addressing modes that are to be found. However, modifications and combinations of these basic modes do exist.

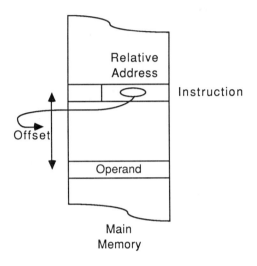

Figure 2.9 Relative Addressing

2.5 Optimising Instruction Formats

Early processors were often capable of operating with only *one* format of instruction. For example, a given processor might have been designed to exhibit a one-and-a-half address format. Of course, whilst many instructions do need (or can be persuaded to make do with) two operands, many need only one. For example, the unary minus operator (negate) has only one operand. Remember that our reason for suggesting a one-and-a-half address format rather than a two address format was that we wished to economise on instruction storage space. We could hardly now claim to have saved instruction storage space if we allow an instruction with only one operand to take the space allowed for a two-operand instruction. It would seem reasonable, then to operate with some form of variable instruction format. In this, the way in which instructions are represented reflects the amount of information that is required to fully describe the operation of the instruction. Usually, a processor exhibiting this type of instruction format allows relatively small areas of memory to be uniquely addressed and accessed. This will either by by accident (the processor's word size is small anyway) or by design (the smallest unit of memory access is less than the processor's word in size). Both the Zilog Z-80 microprocessor and most of IBM's main-frame computers allow memory access in 8-bit units. The Z-80 allows this because it has a word length of 8 bits, whereas the IBM processors may have word lengths of 32 or more bits. In the case of the IBM processors, where the word length is greater than 8 bits, we would call this 8-bit quantity an *8-bit byte*. In both cases, an instruction may be of any length provided it is an integer multiple of 8 bits. In order to simplify our examination of this topic, we will set aside any consideration of IBM main-frame computers and instead concentrate upon the Zilog Z-80 microprocessor and its instruction set. Since the set of instructions that a processor offers depends to a large extent upon its architecture, we must first examine this.

2.6   The Zilog Z-80 Microprocessor

2.6.1   Background

The Z-80 microprocessor was developed by Zilog as an enhanced version of the successful Intel 8080 series of components. In order to maintain software compatability, the Z-80 will execute all of the instructions in the 8080 instruction set. The instruction set of the Z-80 is, however, an expanded version of that of the 8080. This expansion serves to plug a few gaps that it could be argued were left in the 8080 instruction set, whilst at the same time providing a number of instructions required to configure and drive the additional hardware facilities. In the description of the architecture pf the Z-80 that follows, comparisons with the 8080 will only be made where these are of particular significance.

Appendices A and B detail the Z-80, although the reader is introduced to all of the features of the processor that are pertinent to this text.

2.6.2 Architecture

The Z-80 microprocessor is an 8-bit processor that offers direct addressing of 64K of memory and 256 input and output ports. It does this through having 8 data lines and 16 address lines which all appear at the periphery of the integrated circuit. Various control lines, also appearing at the periphery of the chip, allow external devices to determine the direction of data transfers and whether they are destined for somewhere within the 64K memory space or the 256 port input/output space.

As far as the software is concerned, the Z-80 is seen as a number of registers (figure 2.10). It has seven 8-bit general-purpose registers (A, B, C, D, E, H and L) one of which (A) doubles as the special *accumulator*. The remaining six registers may be paired in a prescribed manner (BC, DE and HL) to form three 16-bit registers. In this case, the names B, D and H represent the most-significant halves (bits 15 - 8) of the register pairs. In addition, there is a *flag* register that contains the flag that summarise the results of certain arithmetic and logic instructions. The flags are defined below.

bit 7	*S*	sign	set in the case of a negative result
bit 6	*Z*	zero	set in the case of a zero result
bit 5			is unused
bit 4	*H*	half carry	set when there is a carry from bit 3 to bit 4 (of A)
bit 3			is unused
bit 2	*P/V*	parity/overflow	set when arithmetic overflow occurs or for even parity
bit 1	*N*	negative op'n	set when the previous operation involved a subtraction
bit 0	*C*	carry	set if carry occurred out of the result

Careful study of the instruction set is required to determine exactly when and how the flags are afftected by a given operation. The flag register is paired with the A register (the pair being known as AF) for certain operations. The seven general purpose registers plus the flag register are duplicated (A', F', B', C', D', E', H' and L'). They are accessible by swapping to the *alternate* register set. At that point the previously alternate set becomes the main set and *vice versa*. In this way, the register addressing capability does not have to be doubled. This feature is implemented thus in order to maintain software compatability with the Intel 8080 processor. There are a number of

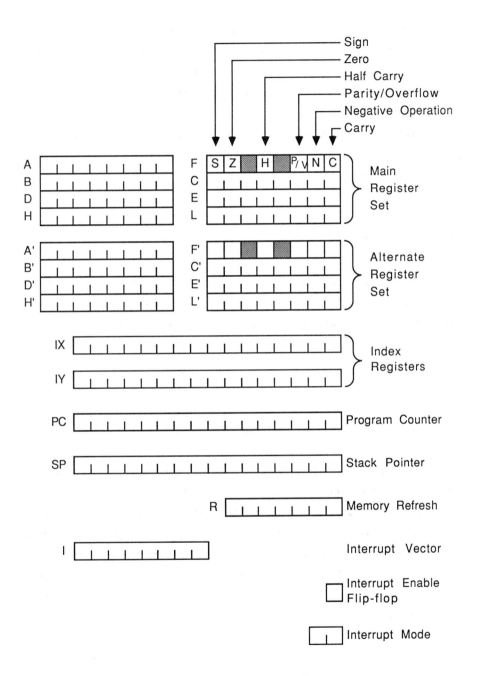

Figure 2.10 Z-80 Register Set

additional registers available directly or indirectly to the program. Among those available directly to the program are two 16-bit *index resisters* (IX, IY) used in certain instructions to provide a form of indexed addressing. Also available directly to the program is the 16-bit stack pointer (SP), a 7-bit register controlling the Z-80's dynamic memory refresh logic (R) and an 8-bit register used in interrupt control (I). Registers not directly accessible to the program, but indirectly affected by the program include the program counter (PC), two interrupt enable flip-flops (IEFF1 and IEFF2) and a 2-bit register defining the current processor interrupt mode (IM).

2.6.3 Instruction Set

The instruction set is given in full in appendix B. The purpose of studying the instruction set at this point is to gain some insight into how it is possible to provide a reasonably complete set of instructions in minimal space. First, though, we will look at the instruction set in general terms. The Z-80 provides instructions for moving 8-bit and 16-bit data:

- from register to register
- from register to memory (direct and indirect)
- from memory to register (direct and indirect).

In addition it provides instructions for the simple arithmetic and logic operations (multiplication and division are not included) and for data shifting and rotating. The arithmetic operations are available on both 8-bit and 16-bit data items, whilst the logic operations may only be performed upon 8-bit data. The final major group of instructions to consider here is the input/output group that allow access to the 256 input or output ports that the Z-80 provides. Other, more minor groups of instructions will be considered elsewhere as the need arises. We can now turn our attention to the structure of the instruction set.

It has already been noted that we could design an instruction set that provides for the possibility of allowing *all* instructions to have space for three memory-based operands. It has also been noted that this is likely to be extremely wasteful of space and memory access time. Instead, we attempt to fit as many instructions as possible into the smallest format (8 bits in the case of the Z-80) and resort to further bits only when necessary. The group of instructions that allow data to be moved from one register to another are (mostly) encoded so as to take up only 8 bits. This is made possible by using two areas or fields of the instruction word to store 3-bit register *addresses*. These refer to each of the seven general purpose registers, leaving one combination spare. This is used to mean (HL), namely *indirect* through HL. The register *addresses* are encoded as follows:

register 0 is B
register 1 is C
register 2 is D
register 3 is E
register 4 is H
register 5 is L
register 6 is (HL)
register 7 is A.

Having taken up six bits with the register operands, there remain only two bits for the op-code. In the case of LD, these two bits are 01. The op-code is placed into bits 7 and 6, the destination register identification into bits 5-3 and the source register identification into bits into bits 2-0. Thus, the instruction

LD A,B   ;copy B to A

will be encoded as

0 1 1 1 1 0 0 0.

If all instructions were encoded using this format, we would have the ability to encode only four different operations, there being only two bits to accomodate the op-code. Of course, the Z-80 has many more than four operation codes. The format which we have seen here is used only for operations that require two register (including (HL)) operands. As soon we move to one operand instructions or those with direct memory references, we find a totally different instruction format. For example, the instruction that places an immediate operand into register D, namely

LD D,35   **;place the number 35 into D**

is encoded as

0 0 0 1 0 1 1 0

with the immediate operand (35 in this case) appearing in the next word.

Note that the code for the destination register (D = 2) appears in the same field as it would for a register to register move, namely bits 5-3. The op-code is in fact spread over bits 7 and 6 *and* 2 - 0. The general operation code for LD r,n being

0 0 r r r 1 1 0,

where *r r r* represents the code for the destination register. Most of the single operand instructions, particularly those with a register operand are encoded in this manner with the op-code *split* over the word.

The remainder of the operations have an op-code that occupied the whole of the word. An instruction like LD A,(1234) that copies the contents of memory location 1234 to the A register has one memory operand and the other in a register. There is only one instruction of this type. We are given no choice of destination register in this instruction and so the whole of the instruction word is available for encoding LD A,(nnnn). In fact, the encoding is

0 0 1 1 1 0 1 0

with the address of the operand (1234 in our example) appearing in the next two words, least significant half first.

Instructions with no operands, like the one that causes a return from a subroutine (RET), are also encoded within all eight bits of the instruction word.

2.7 Getting Going

None of the operations that have been mentioned so far enable us to start a processor doing anything sensible. When power is first applied to a system, nothing may be assumed about the contents of the memory. To all intents and purposes the memory will be filled with garbage. If we simply pointed the program counter at some predefined memory location and set the processor running, the effect would be unpredictable. In order to overcome this, the processor must be started in a particular manner.

On the Z-80 microprocessor, taking the $\overline{RESET}$ input low causes the processor logic to be reset to a predefined state. This includes setting the program counter to 0. Once the $\overline{RESET}$ signal is released the processor starts to execute program from location 0. Unless something meaningful is stored at location 0 onwards, we can see how the unpredictable action mentioned above occurs. We must do something about this.

If our aim is to get an operating system going, and the memory is assumed to contain garbage at switch on, we must place the operating system into the memory. We cannot imagine doing this by some long-winded process that involves writing each word of the program into each successive word of memory. However, we must put *something* into the memory that will run. The solution is to place into the memory a simple program that will read in, from some device, a more complex program. This latter program may be the operating system or it may be a program that will read in the operating system and so on. This process is known as *bootstrapping*.

In modern computers that use this technique, the bootstrap program is placed into some form of read-only memory so that it is always available. A special part of the processor's logic detects a request from the operator to start up the machine and substitutes the bootstrap program instead of normal memory until this feature is released by the software.

Chapter 3

Interconnection Systems

3.1 Introduction

In all computer systems, some level of interconnection between sub-units is required. For example, the processor must be connected to the memory and to the peripheral devices. Some devices need to be connected directly to the memory. In some systems, there is a unique interconnection path (or highway) between each pair of units that need to communicate. This is shown in figure 3.1, where we see that the

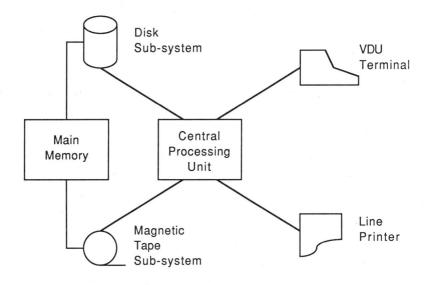

Figure 3.1 Total Interconnection Structure

number of connections is large and therefore the system is expensive. In other systems, a single path interconnects all units. This path is known as a *bus*. In this so called *unified bus* (single bus) approach, any unit wishing to communicate with another must first become *bus master*. Any device may request to become bus master *except memory.* The memory cannot become bus master as it has no need to take it upon itself to initiate a transfer. The unified bus type of structure is shown in figure 3.2.

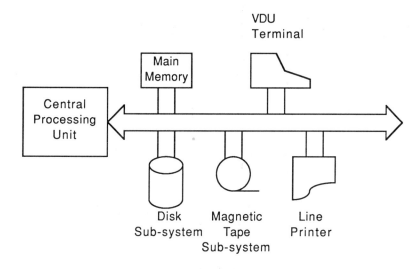

Figure 3.2 Unified Bus Structure

It will be noted that although this type of structure is cheap, it may lead to inefficiencies when, as often happens, two devices wish to use the bus at the same time. In this case, some form of arbitration is required to sort out which device should be the first of the two to gain bus mastership. Comparing this with the total interconnection approach of figure 3.1, we see that here, many transactions can be in progress at the same time. So, we have a conflict of efficiency against cost. The total interconnection system is more efficient in use, but at a greatly increased cost. One solution that has been adopted is to provide a small number of separate busses, each with a particular function. For example, we may have one bus that is dedicated to connecting the processor to the memory, whilst a second bus interconnects all other devices. A third bus may be used to connect certain fast devices directly to the memory. This third bus is for Direct Memory Access (DMA). DMA is described fully in chapter 8 and a typical bus structure is shown in figure 3.3.

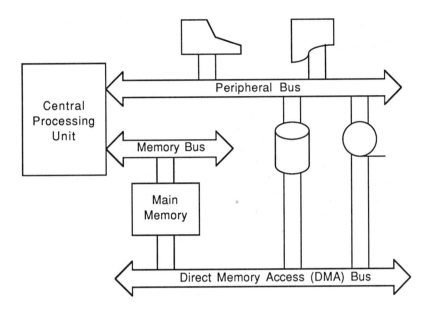

Figure 3.3 Multiple Bus Structure

3.2 Bus Structures

A bus is used to interconnect some or all of the devices in a system to each other and to the processor and memory. In a simple scheme such as we might find being used in a system based on a Z-80 microprocessor, all of the devices are connected together on a single bus. In order to do this, the bus must carry all of the signals that the processor and the devices need in order to communicate with one another. For example, the bus must contain all of the address and data lines so that the processor can identify the memory location of device that it is attempting to contact and then be able to transmit or receive the data. There must be a full set of control lines so that the direction and type of transfer may be identified. Timing signals are also required so that the bus transactions take place at the correct time. Most processors are capable of handling both interrupts and direct memory access (DMA) transfers. The techniques involved are described in detail in later chapters, but it must be noted here that any bus specified for interconnecting such a processor to devices requiring the use of interrupts and DMA must provide the necessary signals.

54

The bus need not necessarily have exactly the same signals as the processor produces. It may be more convenient to modify some of the signals that leave the processor before placing them on to the bus. It may be desirable to introduce new signals on to the bus that the processor produces in some strange way. In order to illustrate this, consider the Z-80 processor. This has a 16-bit address capability and can handle 8 bits of data at a time. It would seem not unreasonable, therefore, to provide 16 address lines and 8 data lines on the bus. The processor also provides two combined direction and timing signals $\overline{RD}$ and $\overline{WR}$. Each of these signals conveys both *direction* and *timing* information. $\overline{RD}$ means "read *now*" and $\overline{WR}$ means "write *now*". On the other hand, many devices that are likely to be connected to the bus might have separate direction and timing signals. The direction signal might be $R/\overline{W}$ (high for read, low for write) and an enable signal, say E. $R/\overline{W}$ obviously gives the direction of the transfer and E may be read as *NOW*. If the majority of devices to be connected to this bus use the latter scheme of separate direction and timing signals, it may be more efficient to construct these signals once and for all between the signals leaving the processor and joining the bus. This can be seen to be straightforward enough when the truth table below is inspected.

$\overline{RD}$	$\overline{WR}$	E	$R/\overline{W}$
0	0	X	X
0	1	1	1
1	0	1	0
1	1	0	X

This shows, given that the combination $\overline{RD}$ and $\overline{WR}$ will never occur, that the timing signal E is simply the NAND of $\overline{RD}$ and $\overline{WR}$. The direction signal $R/\overline{W}$ is simply $\overline{WR}$. We would therefore be tempted to include the logic of figure 3.4 between the processor and the bus. This relieves the individual devices that require $R/\overline{W}$ and E of the task of performing their own translation from one convention to the other. Of course, having decided to modify the signals before placing them on the bus does not preclude us

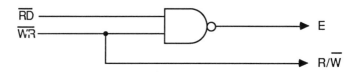

Figure 3.4 Direction and Timing Conversion Logic

from placing the unmodified signals on the bus as well. Thus if some of the devices use one convention for the notification of direction and timing and others use the alternative convention scheme, both are available on the bus. Neither type of device is forced to perform the translation from one convention to the other.

3.3 A Z-80 Bus

In order to see more precisely what might be on a bus, we will construct a bus for a system based on a Z-80 processor. Such a bus might contain at least the following lines:

$$16 \text{ address lines } <A_{15} - A_0>$$
$$8 \text{ data lines } <D_7 - D_0>$$

$\overline{RD}$

$\overline{WR}$

$\overline{MREQ}$ (Memory REQuest)

$\overline{IORQ}$ (Input/Output ReQuest)

Interrupt-related signals

DMA-related signals.

As we have seen, we might well decide to "translate" the $\overline{RD}$ and $\overline{WR}$ signals to E and R/$\overline{W}$ and transmit these along the bus, perhaps alone or perhaps with $\overline{RD}$ and $\overline{WR}$. Similarly, we might choose to transmit MEM/$\overline{IO}$ along the bus instead of or as well as the two address space qualifiers $\overline{MREQ}$ and $\overline{IORQ}$. We will see in later chapters exactly which signals are involved in interrupt and DMA bus transactions.

3.4 Bus Transactions

In order to see how two units on the bus might communicate on such a bus, we will look at two bus transactions. First, we will look at a memory read operation. In this, the processor starts by placing the address of the memory location that it wishes to read on to the address lines. It then asserts $\overline{\text{MREQ}}$ to denote that it is a memory access and $\overline{\text{RD}}$ to denote the direction of the transfer *and* to give the timing of the operation. At this point, the memory starts to locate the data and when it has done so (after a time given by the memory access time), it places the data on to the data lines. At some time (fixed by the processor clock) after the assertion of $\overline{\text{RD}}$, the processor "reads" the data from the data lines. This operation in fact involves the processor simply latching the state of the data lines at some instant in time as dictated by the processor clock. Once the processor has latched the data, it removes the control signals and the address, in response to which, the memory removes the data from the data lines. This sequence is shown more concisely below in terms of distinct processor and memory activity. In the sequence, an arrow between the processor and memory activity columns indicates that the activity at the *blunt* end of the arrow causes or gives rise to the activity shown at the *sharp* end of the arrow. A dashed line within one column denotes a time delay and the cause of the delay is shown in brackets alongside. A semi-colon between two signal names or two activities denotes that the two signals are asserted, to all intents and purposes, simultaneously.

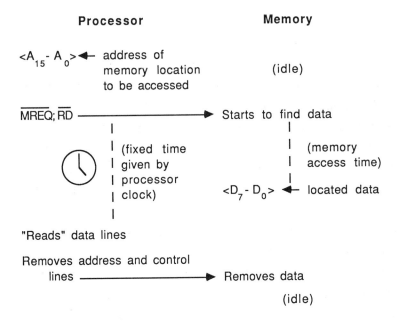

Note that the processor is very much the master in this transaction (even though it is the receiver of data) and the memory is the slave. This is highlighted by the fact that both of the *gives rise to* arrows are from the processor to the memory. Note also that the processor does not assert the signals $\overline{MREQ}$ and $\overline{RD}$ at the same time as the address lines are set up. It leaves a short time between the setting up of the address lines and the assertion of $\overline{MREQ}$ and $\overline{RD}$ to allow for the address lines to *settle* to their intended logic levels.

Let us now consider a memory write operation. This starts off the same as a memory read by the processor placing on to the address lines the address of the memory location to which it wishes to write the data. It also places the data that it wishes to be written on to the data lines. It then asstets $\overline{MREQ}$ and $\overline{WR}$ together to denote a memory access for writing. At this point, the memory starts the process of storing the data. The processor maintains the address, data and control lines for a time given by the processor clock before removing them in readiness for proceeding to the next operation.

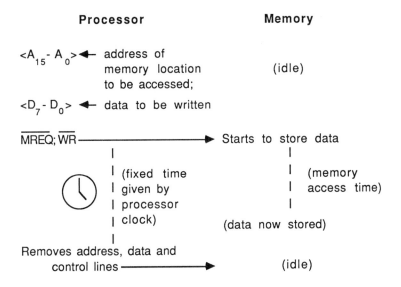

Processor   **Memory**

$<A_{15} - A_0> \leftarrow$ address of
memory location   (idle)
to be accessed;

$<D_7 - D_0> \leftarrow$ data to be written

$\overline{MREQ}; \overline{WR}$ ——————➤ Starts to store data

(fixed time   (memory
given by   access time)
processor
clock)   (data now stored)

Removes address, data and
control lines ——————➤   (idle)

A memory read operation followed by a memory write operation on the same memory location occurs when the processor executes an instruction to increment (add 1 to) the contents of a memory location. The processor reads the contents of the memory location, performs an internal function to increment the number just read and then performs a write operation to replace the incremented number in the memory. Note that this read followed by write sequence is necessary because the memory has no arithmetic capability. On the Z-80, the instruction INC (HL) will perform this operation. If we assume that the register pair HL contains the address *1234*, then this instruction will cause the contents of location 1234 to be incremented. Thus, if location 1234 contained a *5* before the execution of this instruction, it will contain a *6* afterwards. We can see this happening, below, using the same conventions as before.

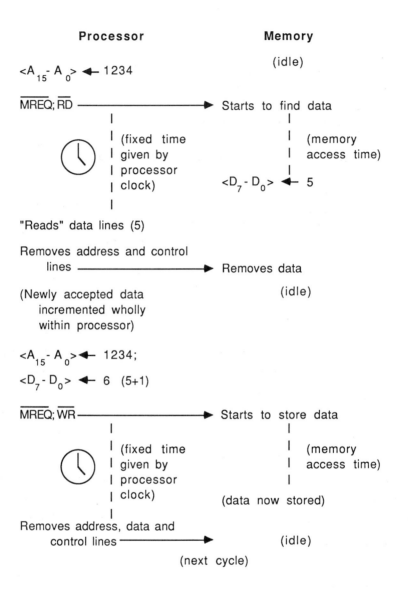

Processor   **Memory**

                                                 (idle)

$<A_{15} - A_0>$ ◄— 1234

$\overline{MREQ}; \overline{RD}$ ————————————► Starts to find data

| | (fixed time | | (memory
| | given by | | access time)
| | processor | |
| | clock) | $<D_7 - D_0>$ ◄— 5
|

"Reads" data lines (5)

Removes address and control
    lines ————————————► Removes data

(Newly accepted data   (idle)
    incremented wholly
    within processor)

$<A_{15} - A_0>$ ◄— 1234;

$<D_7 - D_0>$ ◄— 6 (5+1)

$\overline{MREQ}; \overline{WR}$ ————————————► Starts to store data

| | (fixed time | | (memory
| | given by | | access time)
| | processor | |
| | clock) | (data now stored)
|

Removes address, data and
    control lines ————————————►   (idle)

(next cycle)

Note that we see nothing of the incrementing operation if we look only at the bus. This operation takes place within the processor. Note also that we see the address specifically set to 1234 for the write cycle even though the read cycle was for this address. This is shown because the processor blindly sets the address lines to reflect the address that it wishes to access. It has no idea that the address for the write cycle is the same as that for the read cycle.

It is often useful to see exactly the timing relationships between the various signals on the bus. In order to do so, we often use a *timing diagram*. There are various conventions for drawing a timing diagram and those used here are as follows. When we wish to show a set of similar signals, for example the address lines, we do not bother to show *all* of the lines. In the Z-80, this would mean having to show 16 different signals. Instead, we show the whole group of signals as one. We do this by means of two parallel lines to denote that some of the signals may be high whilst others may be low. The point at which the signals in the group may change (some high to low, some low to high, others unchanged) is denoted by the crossing of the two parallel lines. In showing the change as a cross, we highlight the fact that the change is not instantaneous. We cannot be sure that all of the lines in the group change at *exactly* the same time. This is the reason why the processor allows a settling time before asserting any timing signal such as $\overline{RD}$ or $\overline{WR}$. If the value assumed by a group of signals is known at any point, this is denoted by writing the value between the parallel lines. If the value assumed by a set of lines is undefined, as in the case of the data lines after $\overline{RD}$ but before the memory has located the data and placed it on to the data lines, then this is shown as a dotted pair of parallel lines. Thus, the extract from a timing diagram shown in figure 3.5 denotes that the lines $<D_7 - D_0>$ start to change at the

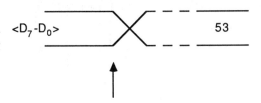

Figure 3.5 Timing Diagram Conventions

point marked by the arrow from an undefined state to holding the value 53. Single signals, such as $\overline{RD}$, are shown as they would appear upon an oscilloscope.

Figure 3.6 shows the timing diagram for the execution of the INC (HL) instruction.

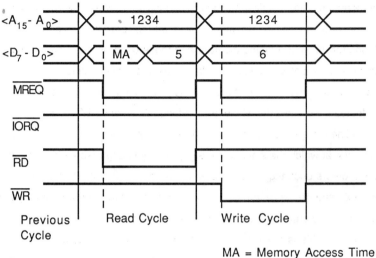

Figure 3.6 Timing Diagram for Z-80 INC (HL) Instruction

3.5 Potential Problems

It has already been noted that the length of the read and write operations - that is the time for which $\overline{RD}$ or $\overline{WR}$ is asserted - is determined by the processor clock. Each operation occupies the same integral number of clock cycles. This kind of operation where everything is linked to the processor clock is known as *synchronous* operation and we call this type of bus a *synchronous bus*.

What happens if the memory access time is greater than the time that the processor allows for a memory access? In the case of a read operation, the processor will attempt to latch the data before it has appeared on the data lines. This means that the processor will read garbage. In the case of a write operation, the processor will remove the data from the data lines before the memory has had chance to store it and the memory will therefore store grabage. In either case, data is corrupted.

If the memory cannot respond within the time allowed by the processor, then the processor has to be held up until the data is ready. We could do this by slowing down the clock so that the time allowed for each of the activities within the processor is increased. This would have the desired effect, but at the expense of speed of operation of the processor and speed of access to other areas of memory and peripheral devices. We need a selective way of slowing access so that we apply the slowing action only to those accesses that need it. The problem is caused by a lack of what is known as *handshaking*. Handshaking is the name given to a technique in which the slave in any transaction replies to every timing signal that is given by the master. This will be described in more detail later, but it is sufficient to note now that this scheme is absent in the Z-80 because the timing of activities on the bus is linked to the processor clock. In order to overcome our problem of slow memory or slow peripheral devices, we need a signal that allows the accessed memory or device to say "Ok, go ahead, the data is there (or has been taken)".

We introduce what might be considered as some form of *negative* handshaking - "hang on, I'm not ready yet". The Z-80 has a signal $\overline{WAIT}$ that does precisely this. When this input is asserted, the processor extends the read or write operation by an integral number of clock cycles. The $\overline{RD}$ or $\overline{WR}$ is held (together with all of the other signals relevant to the transfer) until the end of the clock cycle in which $\overline{WAIT}$ is removed. The memory or device has to insert as many *WAIT states* as it needs to bring the total $\overline{RD}$ or $\overline{WR}$ time to a satisfactory duration relative to the access time of the memory or device. The ability to generate WAIT states is designed into any memory or device that is too slow to respond within the time allowed by the processor. It is provided only when the memory or device is too slow. It is not a dynamic scheme where a particular device sometimes does and sometimes does not assert $\overline{WAIT}$ under the same timing circumstances. It is certainly *not* used to make the processor (and therefore the program) wait for data from, for example, a keyboard.

3.6 The UNIBUS®

The UNIBUS is used on Digital Equipment Corporation's PDP-11 and VAX systems. On most models of PDP-11 all memory and devices are conected by the UNIBUS, but on larger PDP-11s and VAXs only the peripheral devices are connected to the UNIBUS, the memory being on a separate memory bus.

The UNIBUS consists of 56 signals including:

> 18 address lines $<A_{17} - A_0>$
>
> 16 data lines $<D_{15} - D_0>$
>
> Transfer control lines denoting:
>> direction
>>
>> type
>>
>> timing (handshaking)
>
> Interrupt-related lines
>
> DMA-related lines

Note that since the VAX is a 32-bit processor with a 30-bit address space, the UNIBUS is connected to the VAX through an adaptor that performs address mapping and data multiplexing.

The UNIBUS is an asynchronous bus and as such displays full handshaking. Perhaps the best way to describe the basic operation of the UNIBUS is to describe a memory read transaction using the conventions established earlier. The PDP-11 can access either a 16-bit word or an 8-bit byte. The example assumes that a 16-bit word is to be read.

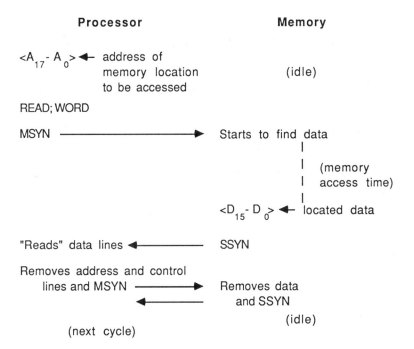

Processor   **Memory**

$<A_{17}$ - $A_0>$ ← address of
                    memory location   (idle)
                    to be accessed

READ; WORD

MSYN ——————————→ Starts to find data
                                        |
                                        | (memory
                                        | access time)
                                        |
                            $<D_{15}$ - $D_0>$ ← located data

"Reads" data lines ←———— SSYN

Removes address and control
    lines and MSYN ————→ Removes data
                    ←————   and SSYN
                                        (idle)
        (next cycle)

The operation is that the processor - the master in this transaction - sets up the address lines to represent the address of the memory location that it wishes to access. It then uses two control lines to select a read operation on a word. After a short settling time, it asserts *MSYN*. This Master SYNchronisation signal informs the selected slave that now is the time for the transfer to start. The selected slave then starts to locate the data as specified by the address lines. As soon as the data is available and placed on to the data lines, the slave asserts *SSYN* (Slave SYNchronisation). This informs the master that the data is now available on the data lines. The master then waits for a short time to ensure that the data lines have setled and then it reads the data by simply latching the data lines into some form of buffer. When the master has done this, it removes the MSYN signal and all of the other signals defining the transfer. In response, the slave removes the data and SSYN.

We can clearly see the handshaking in progress. Every control signal from the master has a reply from the slave. This is evidenced by the fact that there are two *gives rise to* arrows in each direction. We could consider the action of MSYN and SSYN in more human terms, as follows:

Master asserting MSYN means "Please do *xxx* for me"

Slave asserting SSYN   means "Here you are, I've done *xxx*"

Master removing MSYN means "Thank you, I've got that"

Slave removing SSYN   means "You're welcome, have a nice day"

If the selected memory location does not exist, then with the scheme as shown, the processor will wait forever for the SSYN to be returned. We must find a way of ensuring that a reference to a non-existent address does not make the bus and therefore the processor hang up. This is achieved by placing a time limit on the SSYN response to the MSYN. *Bus Control Logic* exists to perform this and other functions. Depending on the exact model of processor, something between 10 and 20μS is allowed after MSYN. If SSYN does not appear within this time, the bus control logic generates a *trap*. This is just like an interrupt, except that it comes from within the processor and not from an external device. In this way, the software (usually an operating system) finds out about the attempted access to a non-existent address. The bus control logic is part of a unit that is logically separate from although physically part of the processor. Its logical separation is due to the fact that the processor is only one of a number of possible bus masters and the bus control logic is responsible also for arbitrating between simultanous requests for bus mastership. It is in fact a *bus arbitrator* as well as a bus controller.

Chapter 4

Memory Interfacing

4.1 Introduction

In the previous chapter we discovered the need for a bus structure to interconnect all of the devices in a system. In this chapter and the next we consider in detail how the memory and peripheral devices in a system are connected to the bus. Note that we talk of them being connected to the bus rather than to the processor because in some cases a peripheral device may wish to access the memory directly without processor intervention.

4.2 Memory Address Decoding

In any situation it is likely that the total amount of memory required in a system will be larger than the amount that is available in a single memory unit, be this unit a single integrated circuit (chip) or a complete memory circuit board. If we are to successfully combine a number of units to produce a memory system that satisfies our requirements, we must ensure that each unit responds to only one range of addresses and that only one unit responds to each address. We need to introduce the ideas of *address decoding*. A logic circuit, known as an address decoder, constantly monitors the address and control lines until it sees a memory address that is within the range that the decoder has been designed to recognise.

Suppose that we wish to construct a read/write memory system that offers 8K x 8-bit words using memory units (chips in this case) of 1K x 8-bit capacity. It is immediately obvious that we need eight memory chips to achieve the desired capacity of our memory system. Let us start by examining a typical memory device of the specified capacity.

4.3 Memory Devices

Firstly, we note that the chip will have a power supply connection and a ground reference connection. In order that we may select any one of the 1024 words within the chip, the chip needs to have ten address lines ($1024 = 2^{10}$). It also needs to have eight data lines. Each of these address and data lines appears as a connection (pin) on the outside of the chip. In order that we may select either a read or a write operation, the chip also requires a direction pin. Let us assume that this pin is labelled R/W (high for read, low for write). Finally, the chip must have a means by which it can be selected independently from the other chips in the memory system. A pin called *chip select* (CS) performs this function and also provides the timing for the transfer. No action takes place within the chip unless CS is asserted. This signal is, more often than not, active-low ($\overline{CS}$). A *logic symbol* for our 1K x 8-bit memory chip is shown in figure 4.1.

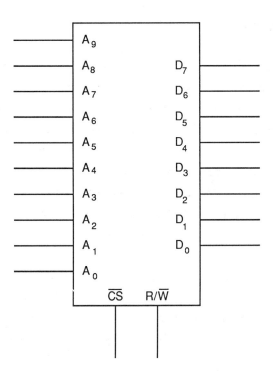

Figure 4.1 Memory Device Block Diagram

4.4 Memory Addressing

Before we can start to design our 8K x 8-bit memory system based upon eight of these devices, we must first establish the range of addresses to which we wish our memory system to respond. Since we know that the memory is 8K in length, we may define the range of addresses simply by selecting the address to which we would like the first word to respond. We call this the *base address* of the memory system. In our example, let us assume that we would like the base address of the memory system to be at address 0. Thus our memory address range is 0 -> (8K - 1). It would seem most convenient if we were to arrange our eight memory devices such that each device serves each successive 1K of the address range as shown in figure 4.2.

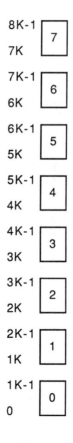

Figure 4.2 Memory Configuration 8K from 1K blocks.

Let us now consider the range of addresses in binary.

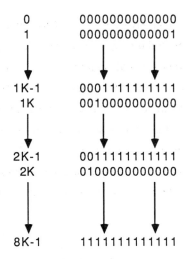

0	0000000000000
1	0000000000001
1K-1	0001111111111
1K	0010000000000
2K-1	0011111111111
2K	0100000000000
8K-1	1111111111111

We note that at each 1K boundary, we see a change in the least significant ten bits from all 1s to all 0s with a simultaneous incrementing of the most significant three bits. Thus the address range 0 -> (1K - 1) can be expressed as

0 0 0 X X X X X X X X X X

where X means "don't care", thus allowing any combination of 0s and 1s in these least significant ten bits. Note that the top three bits give the value 0 which we may take as some form of block number. Since the address range 1K -> (2K - 1) may likewise be expressed as

0 0 1 X X X X X X X X X X

and so on, we can generalise this to

N N N X X X X X X X X X X

where NNN represents the block number (one of eight) in the range 0 - 7.

4.5 Decoder Design

4.5.1 Basic Requirements for a Simple Design

Each chip has ten address pins allowing us to select any one of the 1024 locations within the chip. If we feed the least significant ten address lines into the ten address pins on the chip, then we can see that these are used to select one of 1K locations within *all* of the chips. We must ensure, though, that only one of the chips actually responds. This is where the $\overline{CS}$ pin is used. We select only one of the eight chips in the system as given by the NNN block number in the most significant three bits of the address as shown in the truth table below.

Address lines			Memory $\overline{CS}$ Inputs							
A_{12}	A_{11}	A_{10}	0	1	2	3	4	5	6	7
0	0	0	0	1	1	1	1	1	1	1
0	0	1	1	0	1	1	1	1	1	1
0	1	0	1	1	0	1	1	1	1	1
0	1	1	1	1	1	0	1	1	1	1
1	0	0	1	1	1	1	0	1	1	1
1	0	1	1	1	1	1	1	0	1	1
1	1	0	1	1	1	1	1	1	0	1
1	1	1	1	1	1	1	1	1	1	0

Thus we need to design a circuit that performs the function shown in the truth table. Since this function is used commonly, the logic circuit manufacturers have already produced a single chip that performs the action described by this truth table. The chip (and the action it performs) is known as a *3-to-8 line decoder*. The circuit produces a unique output (one of eight) that is given by the number on the three binary-coded inputs. In the 7400 series of logic circuits, the 74138 provides such a decoder in a single package. In addition to three binary-coded inputs that select an output, the circuit has three *enables* labelled G1, $\overline{G2A}$ and $\overline{G2B}$. The first of these is active-high and the other two are active-low. All of these must be in their active states in order for *any* output to be active. Below is given the function table for the 74138.

Inputs					Outputs							
Enable		Select										
G1	G2	C	B	A	0	1	2	3	4	5	6	7
X	1	X	X	X	1	1	1	1	1	1	1	1
0	X	X	X	X	1	1	1	1	1	1	1	1
1	0	0	0	0	0	1	1	1	1	1	1	1
1	0	0	0	1	1	0	1	1	1	1	1	1
1	0	0	1	0	1	1	0	1	1	1	1	1
1	0	0	1	1	1	1	1	0	1	1	1	1
1	0	1	0	0	1	1	1	1	0	1	1	1
1	0	1	0	1	1	1	1	1	1	0	1	1
1	0	1	1	0	1	1	1	1	1	1	0	1
1	0	1	1	1	1	1	1	1	1	1	1	0

G2 = G2A + G2B

In many of the examples that follow, we tend to enable the decoder with a unique signal and this is often active-low. It is therefore convenient to think of the 74138 as having a single, active-low enable input ($\overline{G}$, say). Figure 4.3(a) shows the logic symbol for the 74138 together with, in (b), a configuration that yields a single enable. Note also that the outputs are, very conveniently for us, active-low. We can thus use the outputs directly to drive the $\overline{CS}$ inputs to the memory devices.

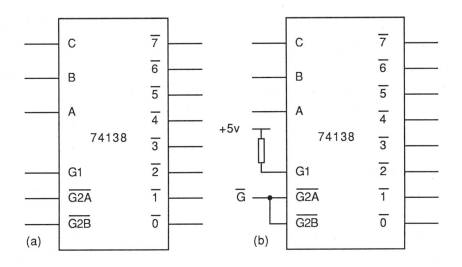

Figure 4.3 74138 3-to-8 line decoder

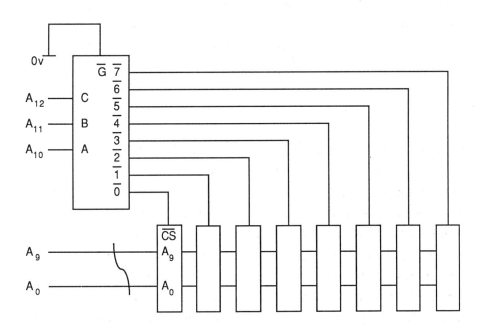

Figure 4.4 8K by 8-bit Memory System from 1K by 8-bit memory components

Having established the existance of the 74138, our required address decoder is very straight-forward. We simply feed the most significant three address bits $<A_{12} - A_{10}>$ to the inputs of a 74138 and connect each of the eight outputs to the $\overline{CS}$ pins on the memory chips. Remember that we must enable the 74138 by forcing our combined enable $(\overline{G})$ low. This we can do by permanently connecting $\overline{G}$ to logic '0' (ground). A complete logic diagram for the decoder is shown in figure 4.4.

Note that not all of the connections to the memory device have been shown. The data lines have been omitted from the diagram for clarity. In fact, the respective data lines on each of the memory chips are connected together to form (part of) the data bus. This violates one of the rules of logic design, namely of not connecting one output to another. In this case, we are allowed to do this because the data outputs of the memory are constructed in a special way. They are *three-state* or *tri-state* outputs. These outputs are capable of being effectively disconnected from the output circuitry inside the chip when the chip is not enabled. In the case of RAM devices, which are capable of being written to as well as read, the data pins on the chip must be capable of giving or receiving data. The must be *bi-directional*.

4.5.1.1   Tri-State and Bi-Directional Devices

The pins on the side of the memory chip must be capable of being connected to the output pins of other memory chips and must, in the case of RAM, be capable of giving and receiving data. The first condition is satisfied by the outputs being *tri-state*. As the name suggests, the output may be in one of three states. These states include the normal two logic states of high and low but have the additional capability of being able to be in an off or *high-impedance* state. Figure 4.5 shows the effective organisation in terms of switches. In this diagram, (a) shows the output in is high state, (b) shows the output in its low state and (c) shows it in the high-impedance state - disconnected from the outside world by means of the switch that is controlled by an enable (E). For our memory, E is derived from $\overline{CS}$. In reality, the output is made from a configuration of transistors and not switches, but this serves as a conceptual idea of the organisation.

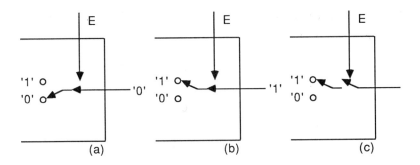

Figure 4.5 Tri-state outputs

In order that the pin on the chip may be capable of accepting data also, another "switch" is used to connect the pin either to the output circuitry or to the input circuitry. The direction of this switch is controlled by the state of the R/$\overline{W}$ input. Figure 4.6 shows this *bi-directional* configuration with output selected in (a) and input selected in (b).

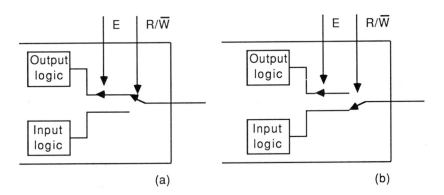

Figure 4.6 Bi-directional configuration typical of memory data connections

4.5.2   A Practical Circuit - Unique Address Decoding

The circuit in its present design allows the memory system of 8K x 8 bits to respond to addresses in the range 0 -> (8K - 1). We have assumed that only thirteen address lines are present. If we were designing this memory system for a processor with more than thirteen address lines, we must think further. In terms of sixteen bit addresses, we construct a new binary address table:

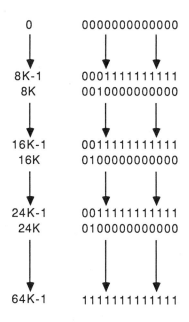

0	0000000000000
8K-1	0001111111111
8K	0010000000000
16K-1	0011111111111
16K	0100000000000
24K-1	0011111111111
24K	0100000000000
64K-1	1111111111111

Bearing in mind that our address decoder looks at only the least significant 13 address lines, we note that the 13-bit address that we are looking for repeats over and over again within the address space defined by 16 address lines. In fact, our memory system responds to addresses in the range 0 -> (8K - 1) and then again to addresses in the range 8K -> (16K - 1), 16K -> (24K - 1) and so on. It responds to eight different address ranges within the 64K address space. This is because we can rewrite the ranges of addresses to which our memory system responds as

X X X 0 0 0 0 0 0 0 0 0 0 0 0 0

to **X X X 1 1 1 1 1 1 1 1 1 1 1 1 1**

where X means *don't care*. The patterns in the least significant thirteen bits - all 8192 of them - repeat for each and every value of XXX. Since there are eight different values of XXX, we see that our memory responds to eight different address ranges. If

we really do wish our memory system to respond *only* to addresses in the range {0 ->
(8K - 1)}, we must modify our address decoder to take into account the three most
significant address bits. It must ensure that it enables the memory system only when
these three address bits are all zero.

We can check for A_{15} - A_{13} being all zero very simply by means of a 3-input NOR gate.
The output of this gate is high *only* when all three inputs are low. We could then use
this output to gate all eight of the $\overline{CS}$ signals before they go to the memory chips. No
memory chip is enabled until the output of the NOR gate is high. This is very expensive
in terms of logic, introducing not only the 3-input NOR gate, but eight inverters to turn
the outputs of the 74138 back to active-high and eight 2-input NAND gates to perform
the gating. Considering again the operation of the 74138, we remember that this has
an active-low enable $(\overline{G})$ that ensures that no output will be active unless $\overline{G}$ is low. We
may therefore feed the output of our 3-input NOR gate (high when A_{15} - A_{13} are all
zero) to the composite $\overline{I}$ input of the '138, having first inverted it, of course. Thus our
modified design is shown in figure 4.7. This form of address decoding, where the
decoder responds to only one specific address range, is known as a *unique address
decoder*. Previously, we had designed a *non-unique address decoder*.

If we now need a memory system to respond to addresses in the range 8K -> (16K -1),
we can see how to do this. Since we can write this address range as

0 0 1 X X X X X X X X X X X X X

we can see that we need to ensure that the 74138 is enabled *only* when A_{15} and A_{14}
are both zero and A_{13} is one. We can do this very simply by inverting A_{13} on its way to
the 3-input NOR gate. Since the NOR gate will produce a high only when all of its
inputs are low, we can see that the only pattern on A_{15} - A_{13} that can produce three
lows on the inputs is that for which we are searching. In this way, we could design
unique address decoders that allow an 8K x 8-bit memory system to reside on *any* 8K
address boundary, but unfortunately we would require up to eight different designs!

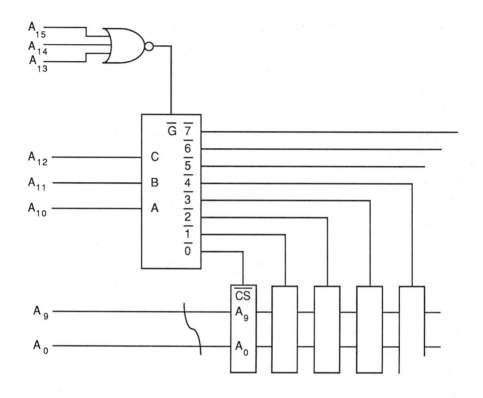

Figure 4.7 Modifications required for Unique Address Decoding

In a general purpose computer system, it is often necessary to add memory to the system as the demand for computing power grows in the organisation. In order to cater for this need, the manufacturers produce memory units upon printed circuit boards that are very similar to our 8K x 8-bit memory system (although they are likely to have a greater capacity!). It would be very costly for the manufacturer to produce a range of boards that are identical in all respects apart from the decoding of a few of the upper address lines. Instead, they produce a single board that is reconfigurable either by means of wired links on the board or by means of simple on/off switches. This has a further advantage that a single spare board may be held on site that can be slotted into any memory address range to replace a faulty memory board. We will now see how this may be achieved by considering the design of a *single* address decoder that will allow the 8K x 8-bit memory system to reside on any 8K boundary.

Firstly we must investigate how we can use a wired link or a simple on/off switch to produce logic levels. We may consider either since they are electrically identical. A closed switch is equivalent to a made wire link, whilst an open switch is exactly the same as a broken wire link. If we place a switch between any input to a normal logic gate and ground and then close the switch, the input thus connected will see exactly 0 volts. This is a logic '0'. If we open the switch, the input voltage *floats* up to some arbitrary level below the supply voltage (5 volts). The logic gate may see this as a logic '1' but may not. In order to ensure that it sees a logic '1', we place a resistor of about 1K (1000 ohms) between the input and the supply voltage. This is exactly what we do with any other input that we wish to hold permanently high. If we now close the switch, the input still sees a logic '0' and the small current that flows through the resistor does no harm. Thus if we connect our switch and resistor as shown in figure 4.8, we can produce a logic '0' if we close the switch and a logic '1' if we open the switch.

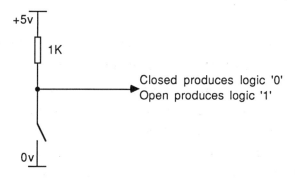

Figure 4.8 Obtaining Logic Levels from a simple on/off Switch

Having decided that we can reliably produce logic levels from switches or wired links, we now look for a logic gate that acts as a comparator - some sort of "same as" gate. The exclusive-OR gate fits the bill precisely. The output of a 2-input exclusive-OR gate is high only when the two inputs are different. When the two inputs are the same, therefore, the output is low. Below is shown the logic symbol and truth table for a 2-input exclusive-OR gate.

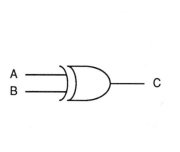

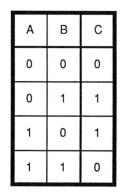

A	B	C
0	0	0
0	1	1
1	0	1
1	1	0

Thus if we connect the *output* of a switch to one of the two inputs of an exclusive-OR gate and an address line to the other, we have a comparator for a single address line. If the state of the address line matches that of the switch, the output of the gate will be low, otherwise it will be high.

In our particular example, we need three switches - one for each address line comparison. Let us label them S_{15} - S_{13} in order to easily denote which address line is decoded by each switch. If we now connect three exclusive-OR gates as above, we have a situation where the outputs of all three gates will be low only when the pattern on the address lines matches that specified by the switch settings. We may now use a 3-input NOR gate to detect when all three exclusive-OR outputs are low. The NOR gate will, in this case, produce a high output. This may be inverted and then used to enable the 74138 so that it functions and produces an output *only* when the pattern on the upper address lines matches that set upon the switches. A diagram for this newly modified part of the address decoder circuit is shown in figure 4.9.

We must now consider what we tell the *user* of this address decoder. In this case, the user will be the person who is responsible for configuring the address decoder to select the addresses to which this memory system is to respond in a particular system. We have noted that the exclusive-OR gate produces a low output when the two inputs are the same and it is this state that our 3-input NOR gate detects. Thus we, as designers, know that we have to set the switch to produce a logic '0' when we wish to have the decoder look for a 0 on the associated address line. Thus we can tell the user that the switch associated with a given address line must be *closed in order to*

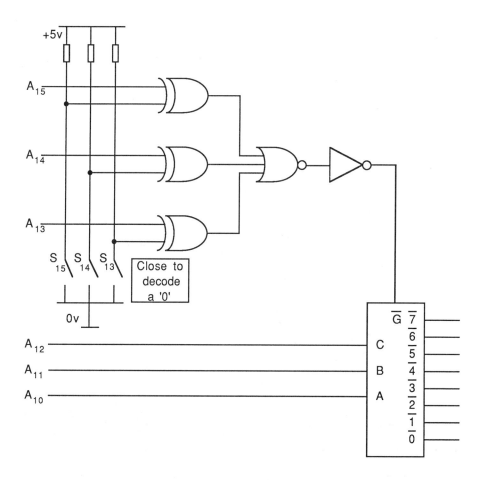

Figure 4.9 Modifications for Switch Selectable Address Decoding

decode a '0'.' We are, perhaps, more used to associating the closure of a switch with *on* or logic '1', but in this case we know that the switch produces a logic '0' on closure. Remember that the exclusive-OR gate produces a high output when the two inputs differ. If we then take the outputs of the three exclusive-ORs and feed them to a 3-input NAND gate instead of a NOR gate, we have produced a circuit that looks for all of the exclusive-OR outputs to be high. This happens when, in each case, the two inputs differ. Thus we can now tell the user that a switch must be *closed to decode a '1'* on the associated address line. There is an added bonus in this case. The 3-input NAND gate produces a low output when all three inputs are high and the 74138 requires an active-low enable. We can therefore dispense with the inverter that was required in the previous circuit. Further modifications to our circuit are shown in figure 4.10. Note that is vitally important to include the instruction "close to decode a '1'" in the diagram.

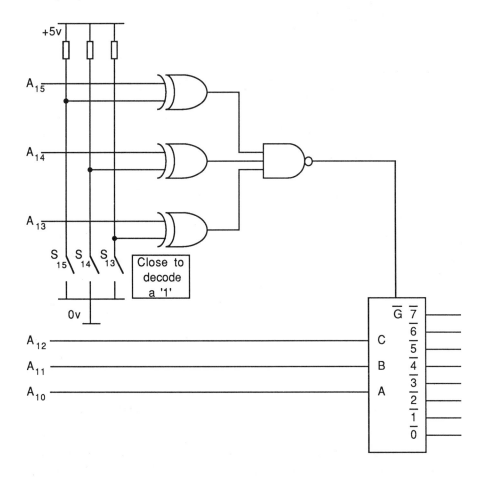

Figure 4.10 Further Modifications to the Circuit for More Ergonomic Operation

An alternative approach to that above would have been to use exclusive-*NOR* gates (output *low* when inputs differ) and continue to feed the outputs into a NOR gate. However, the solution adopted is more economical in terms of gates used due to the ommission of the inverter.

4.5.3 Minimal Address Decoding

Until now, we have been considering the design of memory systems for general purpose systems. In many situations in which a microprocessor is used, the program that is to run is always the same. We call this type of system a *dedicated system*. Once this program has been debugged, it can be relied upon to function correctly and to never attempt to address areas of memory that it should not. In this case, we may not need to provide unique address decoding. In systems where cost is a very important factor - for example washing machine controllers, motor vehicle applications - the address decoding may be very simple indeed. Imagine a system where the memory requirement is for two areas of memory. The first, located at address 0 onwards, is for a 4K Read-Only Memory (probably EPROM). The second, located at address 8K onwards is for an 8K block of Random Access (read/write) Memory. As before, we start by writing out the address ranges, assuming a processor with a 16-bit address capability.

4K block at 0 -> (4K - 1): 0 0 **0** 0 X X X X X X X X X X X X X

8K block at 8K -> (16K - 1): 0 0 **1** X X X X X X X X X X X X X

The first point worthy of note is that the number of *don't care* address bits in the 4K address range is obviously less than that in the 8K block. We require twelve bits to address any one of 4K different locations whereas we need thirteen bits to address 8K. A further point to note is that the address bit that always differs from one address range to the other is address bit 13. It is always 0 in the range 0 -> (4K - 1) and always 1 in the range 8K -> (16K - 1). If we assume an active-low enable to each of the two blocks of memory, our address decoder could be as simple as a single inverter placed on address bit 13. Figure 4.11 shows this in operation. A_{13} is connected directly to the active-low enable on the 4K Read-Only section of the memory so that it is enabled when A_{13} is low. The inverse of A_{13} is connected to the active-low enable on the 8K RAM section so that this is enabled when A_{13} is high.

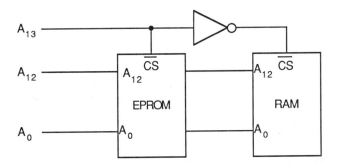

Figure 4.11 Simple, non-unique Address Decoder for a Minimal System

Of course, if the program attempted to access address

$$0 1 0 0 0 0 1 1 0 1 0 0 1 1 1 0$$

then the Read-Only section would respond, address 001101001110 being the one actually selected. But, we have already noted that the program is fully debugged and is assumed to never access memory erroneously. We could easily give this memory system unique address decoding by any one of a number of means, but this would not help in a dedicated system such as we are imagining. If the program does attempt to access an address that does not actually exist, then it has obviously failed in some way due either to a hardware or software fault. We could arrange for no memory access to take place by introducing unique address decoding, but the program will be unaware of this. It will simply carry on executing program that it obvioulsy was not intended to execute.

4.5 Memory in Larger Systems

At the other end of the scale of computer system size and complexity, most large systems have some form of *memory management* system that allows for easy and reliable sharing of memory between a number of programs residing simultaneously within the system. In this case, the address produced by the program - the *virtual* address - is *mapped* into an address that is used to actually access the memory - the *real* address. The virtual to real address mapping is carried out by the memory mapping hardware acting upon instructions from the *operating system*. In some techniques employing this *virtual memory* approach, the number of bits in the virtual address may differ from that in the real address. If the number of bits in the real address exceeds the number of bits in the virtual address, we can see that this gives us an opportunity to accomodate a number of programs in the real memory simultaneously. If, on the other hand, the number of bits in the virtual address exceeds that in the real address, we can perhaps imagine that we could fit into the memory a program larger than the memory! The techniques of *segmentation* and *paging* both display these characteristics.

Chapter 5

Peripheral Interfacing

5.1 Device Controllers

Any peripheral device is connected to the system via some sort of *device controller* or *interface*. For example, each VDU terminal in a system will be connected through a device controller, such as a serial interface. This converts the data presented to it by the processor along the bus in parallel form into the serial bit stream required by the terminal. Another example might be of a group of similar disk drives being collected together and connected to the bus by a single controller.

As far as the program is concerned, a device appears as one or more registers. A simple device like a serial interface may be seen by the program as only two registers whilst a complex interface like a disk controller may appear as eight or more registers.

5.1.1 A Real Device - The 6850 ACIA

In order to give an idea of how this works in practice, we will look briefly at the hardware and software aspects of the *6850 ACIA* (Asynchronous Communications Interface Adaptor). This is an example of a serial interface as mentioned above. It may be considered as two devices in one. The first is responsible for the transmission of data along a serial line and the second receives data from another serial line. In hardware terms, it consists of a parallel to serial converter on the transmitter side and a serial to parallel converter on the receiver side. The 6850 is accessed by program through four registers that respond to two addresses. As a result, the 6850 has only one *address* input and this it calls RS (Register Select). The four registers are in two pairs and it is each pair that responds to each address. The distinction between the registers in each pair is made by whether the 6850 is being read or written to since two of the registers are read only whilst the other two are write only. Whether the 6850 is being read or written to is determined by the state of the single direction signal R/$\overline{W}$. This is high for read and low for write. The four registers are:

(i) the status register (read only),

(ii) the control register (write only),

(iii) the receive (input) data register (read only)

and (iv) the transmit (output) data register (write only).

The layout of the four registers is best expressed diagramatically:

	R/$\overline{W}$ = 0	R/$\overline{W}$ = 1
RS = 0	Control Register	Status Register
RS = 1	Transmit Data Register	Receive Data Register

The 6850 is selected by a combination of chip select signals. There are three chip selects, C S 0 and C S 1 are active-high and $\overline{CS2}$ is active-low. All three of the chip selects must be in their active state in order for the 6850 to be selected. The overall timing of the operations on the 6850 is given by the E (enable, active-high) signal.

Appendix C presents a more complete description of the 6850 ACIA than is possible or necessary here.

5.2 Accessing the Controllers - a Choice

The device registers will be accessed by the program in one of two ways. In the first of these two ways they will behave as though they are normal memory locations. The device addresses occupy space in the memory address space. Peripheral devices behaving in this way are known as *memory-mapped* devices. They may be accessed by *any* memory referencing instruction. The alternative access method involves a separate set of instructions specifically directed at input and output. These instructions allow access to a second address space that contains all of the device registers. Devices addressed in this way are known as *port input/output* devices.

Some processors offer a choice of either memory-mapped or port input and output whilst others only offer the memory-mapped type. We can detect whether a particular processor offers port input and output by simply inspecting its instruction set. If it has no instructions that are specifically designed for input and output then it obviously offers no port input/output facilities. When a processor does have input and output instructions, we are not bound to use them and therefore port input/output since it will have, by definition, a memory address space that we can encroach upon for our memory-mapped input and output devices. The PDP-11 is an example of a processor that has no specific input or output instructions and therefore all of its input and output is memory mapped. The Z-80, on the other hand, does have a set of input and output instructions and therefore offers both techniques. The actual decision as to whether we use one technique or the other, when a choice exists, depends upon a number of factors.

5.2.1 Memory Mapped vs Port Input/Output

In the previous section we saw how the choice of whether to use memory-mapped or port input/output may be made for us. In the case of the PDP-11, there is no choice at all. The porcessor offers *only* memory-mapped input/output because of its architecture. In the case of the Z-80, however, there is a genuine choice.

Memory-mapped input/output is likely to be chosen for its ability to access device registers as though they are memory addresses. This is likely to make for efficient programming. Imagine a device controller in which the action of the controller is started by writing a '1' to a particular bit. Most controllers on the UNIBUS have this feature and in order to maintain consistency, any such *GO* bit is always positioned in bit 0 of the register. Provided the GO bits always reads back as a '0' and this is indeed the case, an instruction to increment the contents of the register will cause the GO bit to be set. Thus we have set the GO bit with a single instruction execution. If the register was interfaced in a port input/output manner, the contents of the port would have to be read into a processor register, bit 0 would have to be set within the processor and the result sent back to the register - all of this taking more time than the previous method. There are, however, situations in which the programming required for port input/output is more efficient than that required for memory-mapped input/output. In most cases, though, programs written for memory-mapped devices are more efficient. Memory-mapped input/output does have its disadvantages, though.

In order to allow a number of device registers to appear as memory locations, we must set aside part of the memory address space for these registers. This has the obvious effect of reducing the amount of memory that we can attach to a system. We will see later how the effect of this can be minimised, but in any case some of the memory address space will be lost. This may preclude us from using memory-mapped input/output where the memory address space is likely to be required for real memory and is therefore at a premium.

5.3 Address Decoding

In either case, the device is connected to the bus and must be constantly looking on the bus for (one of) its own address(es). Each device contains an *address decoder* that performs this function. We have already seen the basic principles of address decoding, but we now must examine the hardware differences between the two techniques of memory-mapped and port input/output interfacing and see how this influences our design for an address decoder.

5.3.1 Memory Mapped Address Decoding

When designing a memory address decoder for a memory-mapped device, we follow the same basic principles as for a memory address decoder. The only difference is that in the case of the memory-mapped device we are decoding for a smaller number of addresses. It would be unreasonable for us to choose addresses within the memory address space that are occupied by memory. The only way that we could do this safely is to modify our memory address decoder to ignore some of the addresses. Instead, we assign our device addresses within an unused area of the memory address space. Of course, many systems are put together from a number of memory and peripheral components and it is often impossible to predict, at the design stage, exactly how much memory and how many devices of what type are to be placed into a system. It is therefore difficult to predict exactly where the gaps in the memory complement will be. One solution to this is to adopt a convention for a given system that places all of the memory-mapped devices into one area of the memory address map. A commonly adopted convention is to dedicate the upper 256 locations of the memory address map to the devices. Thus all devices have an address in the range $FF00_{16}$ to $FFFF_{16}$. It will be noted that in this range, all of the top eight bits of the address are ones and it is the lower eight bits that select the actual device register that is being addressed. On the PDP-11, a larger area of the memory address space is set aside for the peripheral devices. In fact, it is the upper 4K (words) of the address space that is used for this purpose. Let us concentrate on the Z-80, though, and adopt the convention mentioned above.

When the Z-80 wishes to make an access to a memory location it places the address of the memory location on to the 16 address lines. After a short settling time it asserts the control signals that give the direction and timing information ($\overline{RD}$ or $\overline{WR}$) and $\overline{MREQ}$ (Memory REQuest) to denote that it is a memory access that is required. Thus if we wish to design an address decoder that will serve a memory-mapped device as defined by our convention above, we need to consider the following. We must look for the most-significant eight address lines ($<A_{15} - A_8>$) to be high and for the least significant to carry the defining address. We must also look for $\overline{MREQ}$. We have already seen that some devices may appear as more than one register. This means that our address decoder must therefore be capable of responding to more than one address. We will assume that these addresses are *contiguous* (follow one another).

As an example, we will consider the design of an address decoder for a *6850 ACIA* that will allow the 6850 to respond to the two memory-mapped addresses $FF02_{16}$ and $FF03_{16}$.

We start our design by writing down the two addresses in binary:

$$\text{FF02}_{16} \quad \textbf{1 1 1 1 1 1 1 1} \quad \textbf{0 0 0 0 0 0 1 0}$$

$$\text{FF03}_{16} \quad \textbf{1 1 1 1 1 1 1 1} \quad \textbf{0 0 0 0 0 0 1 1}$$

We immediately notice that the only difference between these two addresses is in bit 0. This is low for FF02_{16} and high for FF03_{16}. We can therefore write both addresses at once as:

$$\text{FF02/3}_{16} \quad \textbf{1 1 1 1 1 1 1 1} \quad \textbf{0 0 0 0 0 0 1 X}$$

We notice also that the difference between the two pairs of registers in the 6850 is the state of the RS input. This is low for the control and status pair and high for the data pair. Thus it would seem sensible to feed A_0 directly into RS in order to select one of the two pairs. In this way, FF02_{16} will address the control and status pair and FF03_{16} will address the data pair. This means that we now have only to recognise the most significant 15 bits of the address. Of these, the most significant eight and A_1 must all be high and $<A_7 - A_2>$ must be low. $\overline{\text{MREQ}}$ must also be low. Before we can complete the design, we must consider the question of direction and timing. The Z-80 uses two signals, $\overline{\text{RD}}$ and $\overline{\text{WR}}$, each of which convey *both* direction and timing information whereas the 6850 uses two separate signals R/$\overline{\text{W}}$ and E. We have already seen a circuit in figure 3.4 that will convert from one standard to another. This involves simply NANDing the two signals $\overline{\text{RD}}$ and $\overline{\text{WR}}$ to produce E and taking $\overline{\text{WR}}$ to R/$\overline{\text{W}}$. We therefore include this in our final design. The full logic circuit for this address decoder is shown in figure 5.1. Note that we take full advantage of the logic within the 6850 that combines the three separate chip select inputs C S 0, C S 1 and $\overline{\text{C S 2}}$. It is as though there is inside the 6850 a *free* 2-input NAND gate combining C S 0 and C S 1 followed by a 2-input NOR gate combining the output of the NAND gate with $\overline{\text{C S 2}}$. Our circuit produces three separate logic levels that are combined inside the 6850 in this way. We must ensure that *all* of these inputs are active before the 6850 will respond.

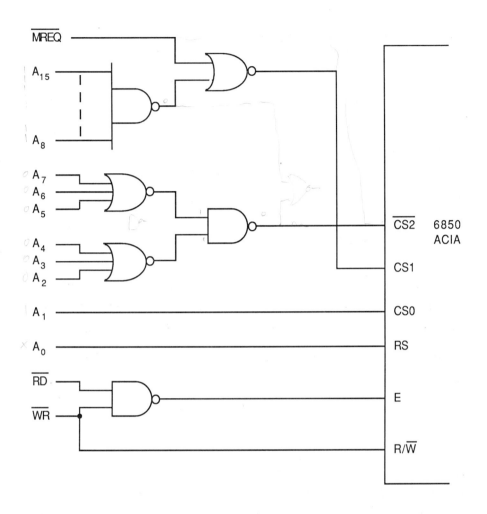

Figure 5.1 Address decoding for 6850 ACIA as Memory Mapped device

5.3.2 Input/Output Port Address Decoding

We now move on to see what happens when the Z-80 executes on of the instructions dedicated to input and output. The Z-80 has two basic operation codes for input and output. Input is performed with the *IN* instruction and output with the *OUT* instruction. There are a number of forms of each instruction, each form being represented in both the IN and OUT instructions. The basic forms of the IN and OUT instructions are

```
IN        A,(n)    ;input from port n to the A-register
```

```
and       OUT      (n),A    ;output to port n from the A-register.
```

In both cases, n is an 8-bit constant that represents the *port number*. This is placed on to the least significant eight address lines as the instruction is executed, together with $\overline{RD}$ or $\overline{WR}$ depending on whether it is an IN or an OUT instruction that is being executed, respectively. In order to distinguish this bus transaction from that of a memory (or memory-mapped device) access, the signal $\overline{IORQ}$ (active-low Input/Output ReQuest) is also asserted. The state of the most significant eight address lines may be normally be ignored in decoder design, although in the Z-80 their state is well defined for each of the IN and OUT instruction variants. For the basic IN and OUT instructions $<A_{15} - A_8>$ carry the contents of the A-register. In the variants in which the port number is specified by the contents of register C, $<A_{15} - A_8>$ carry the contents of the B-register. For completeness, a full set of Z-80 IN and OUT instructions and the state of the eight most significant address lines in each case is given in the Z-80 instruction set in appendix B.

If we wish to modify our 6850 address decoder that previously responded as a memory-mapped device (figure 5.1) to now respond to *port* addresses 2 and 3, we must design a decoder that looks at address lines $<A_7 - A_1>$ and $\overline{IORQ}$. A_0 is still fed directly to the RS input on the 6850 in order to select between the control and status registers on port 2 and the data registers on port 3. The logic diagram for such a decoder is shown in figure 5.2. It is worth noting that this circuit is simpler than that for the memory-mapped device due to the fact that we have included no reference to the most significant address lines $<A_{15} - A_8>$. This is due to the fact that, as stated above, these lines are in most cases undefined. It is possible, however, to include these lines both from the hardware and software points of view. This is likely to be the case only in very specialised or dedicated systems. The fact that the general circuit is less complex may be a reason for choosing port input/output in preference to memory-mapped input/output when taken in conjunction with the comments of section 5.2.1.

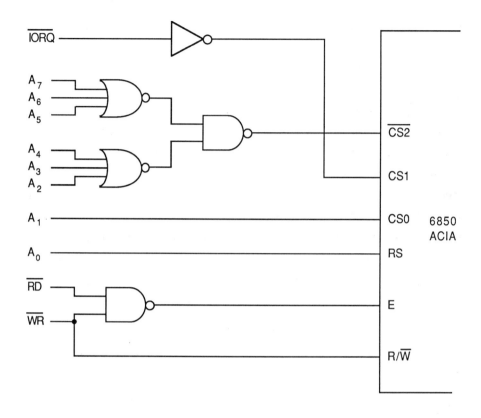

Figure 5.2 Address decoding for 6850 ACIA as Port Input/Output device

5.3.3 Selecting the Address

It is often the case that a system will contain more than one interface of the same type. Each interface may be contained on a single module or printed circuit board and we may include a number of interfaces in a system by simply including the required number of boards. In this case, we would need each board to respond to a different address otherwise the program would be unable to distinguish one interface from another. We could achieve this by designing and building a number of boards, each responding to a different address. This would be very wasteful of the design and manufacturing resources of a company. Instead, we would design a board that can be configured to respond to any address (or address range in the case of multi-register devices). The address(es) to which the device is to respond could ideally be set up on a small bank of switches as part of this *variable* or *switch-selectable* address decoder.

In the case of our 6850 address decoder, we might wish to redesign it so that it will respond to *any* pair of memory addresses (even + next odd address) in the range $FF00/1_{16}$ - $FFFE/F_{16}$ as specified by a set of switches. We can see from our previous design that we need to look for $<A_{15} - A_8>$ to be all high and for $\overline{MREQ}$ to be low. We should still connect A_0 directly to RS in order to select the appropriate register pair (control and status pair or data pair) and we still need our sub-circuit to derive the direction and timing signals $R/\overline{W}$ and E. The address is to be selected by a set of switches. As we have already dealt with address lines $<A_{15} - A_8>$ and A_0, we only have left the seven address lines $<A_7 - A_1>$. These seven address lines allow us to select one of 128 (2^7) places at which these two registers may appear. This helps to confirm that we have the correct number of bits in the decoder. Since we have seven address lines to check, we need seven switches to allow the address to which the decoder is to respond to be specified. We also need a logic gate that can look for *same as* or *different to*. This gate is the *exclusive-OR* gate. Remember that the exclusive-OR gate produces a high output when one or the other, but not both, inputs are high. We must therefore feed to seven exclusive-OR gates the seven address lines $<A_7 - A_1>$ together with the outputs from seven switches. As with the equivalent variable address decoder for memory, in order minimise cost, we elect to use single pole, single way (on/off) switches. Reference to figure 4.6 will remind the reader of the way in which switches may be configured to produce logic outputs. The outputs from the seven exclusive-OR gates are fed to a NAND gate whose output goes low only when all of the inputs are high. This occurs when all of the exclusive-OR gates detect that their two inputs are different. As before, this means that if we wish the decoder to look for a high on a particular address line, we must provide a low from the corresponding switch. This occurs when the switch is closed and so we must denote our switches "close to decode a 1". This is, perhaps, the most natural way for us to think and therefore the most *ergonomic* choice to make. The full circuit diagram is shown in figure 5.3.

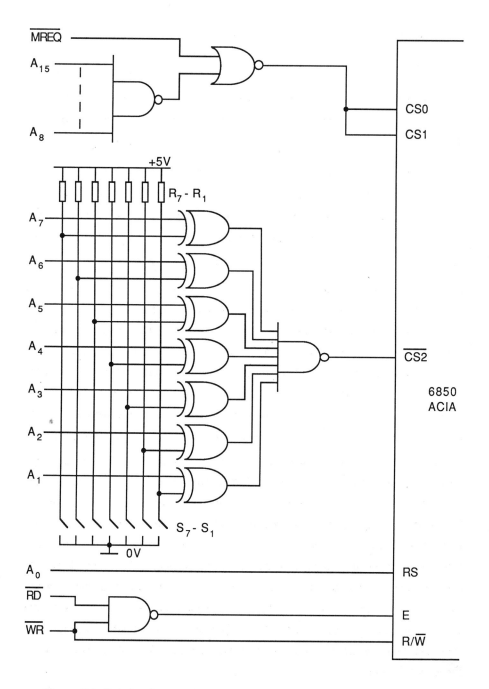

Figure 5.3 Switch selectable Memory Mapped address decoder for 6850 ACIA

The inclusion of seven exclusive-OR gates in our circuit begins to make the circuit look rather cumbersome. The combination of these exclusive-OR gates and the NAND gate consitutes a 7-bit *digital comparator*. This function of digital comparison is a commonly required function and because of this, the manufacturers of integrated circuits have now produced a digital comparator on a single integrated circuit. The *25LS2521* is an 8-bit digital comparator with an active-low enable. Its logic circuit is shown in figure 5.4. As can be seen, each of the A inputs must be the same as its equivalent B input *and* the enable input ($\overline{\text{Ein}}$) must be low. When all of these conditions are met, the

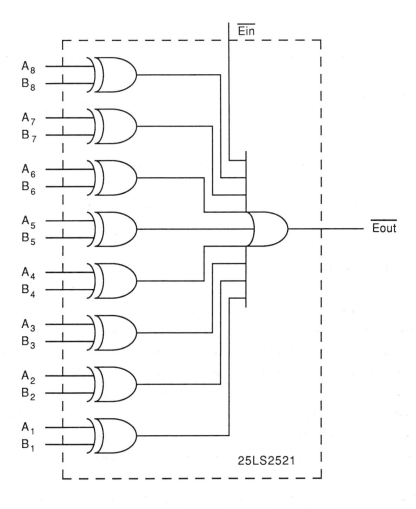

Figure 5.4 8-bit Digital Comparator (25LS2521)

active-low output $\overline{Eout}$ goes low. The inclusion of the 25LS2521 in our circuit drastically reduces the component count. The revised logic diagram is shown in figure 5.5. The eighth A/B pair of inputs on the 25LS2521 are used to check the state of the most significant eight address lines by comparing the output of the 8-input NAND gate with a fixed low (GND). Note that we no longer fully utilise the internal logic of the 6850 that combines $CS0$, $CS1$ and $\overline{CS2}$. We only use the active-low $\overline{CS2}$ input and therefore force the other two, active-high inputs $CS0$ and $CS1$ to their required high state with a pull-up resistor (R8) to the supply. Since the 25LS2521 has inside it the equivalent of eight exclusive-NOR gates (exclusive-ORs with inverted outputs) all feeding their outputs together with the inversion of $\overline{Ein}$, we have to rethink the notation of the address selection switches. In our previous circuit, we chose to configure the address switches so that we could label them "close to decode a 1". However, the 25LS2521 looks for each of the A/B input pairs to match and so we are forced, without the inclusion of extra logic, to adopt this. The result of this is that we need to take the normal logic levels from the switches, namely closed for '0', open for '1'. We must therefore relabel our switches as "close to decode a 0". This is perhaps less ergonomic than the previous configuration, but it is not uncommon to have to pay some price for the reduction in component count and circuit complexity.

5.3.4 Selecting the Access Type

Having decided to produce an interface that may be placed at any one of a number of addresses, we could extend this flexible approach by designing our board so that it can be configured to respond *either* as a memory-mapped device *or* as a port I/O device. This would almost certainly be the case in a commercial design where the choice of access type is left to the purchaser without the manufacturer having to produce a number of designs or restricting the purchaser once the purchase has been made. The slight increase in complexity that will be apparent is probably a price worth paying both by the manufacturer and the purchaser - an uncommon situation.

The board could be instructed as to which way to respond by means of a further switch. We have so far used seven switches in our design and it is interesting to note that the

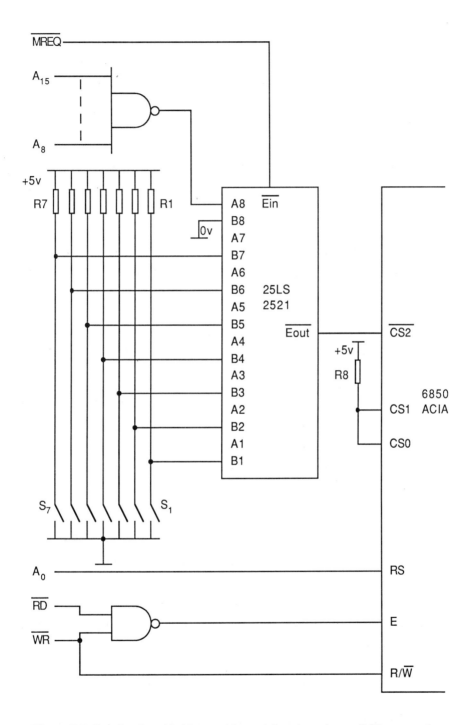

Figure 5.5 Switch selectable Memory Mapped decoder using an 8-bit comparator

type of switch bank that we would probably choose in fact would have eight switches upon it. We could use the eighth as a *mode switch* to select whether our decoder is to respond as a memory-mapped device or as a port. We will start by trying to write a logic expression to define the action of our new decoder. We need the 6850 to be selected when either:

(i)   the decoder has been instructed to act as a memory-mapped device and the current bus transaction is a memory access *and* the address on the bus matches the address on the switches

or (ii)   the decoder has been instructed to act as a port device *and* the current bus transaction is a port access *and* the address on the bus matches the address on the switches.

This can now be written more precisely as a logic expression using as inputs the elements that we know are easy to achieve, for example, $<A_{15} - A_8> = 1$s:

$$6850 \text{ enable} = ((\text{mode} = \text{mem}) \text{ \& } \overline{\text{MREQ}} \text{ \& } (<A_{15} - A_0> = 1s) \text{ \& } (<A_7 - A_1> = <S_7 - S_1>))$$
$$+ ((\text{mode} = \text{port}) \text{ \& } \overline{\text{IORQ}} \text{ \& } (<A_7 - A_1> = <S_7 - S_1>))$$

We can simplify this expression having spotted the common term $(<A_7 - A_1> = <S_7 - S_1>)$. It now becomes:

$$6850 \text{ enable} = (<A_7 - A_1> = <S_7 - S_1>) \text{ \& } (((\text{mode} = \text{mem}) \text{ \& } \overline{\text{MREQ}}$$
$$\text{ \& } (<A_{15} - A_8> = 1s)) + ((\text{mode} = \text{port}) \text{ \& } \overline{\text{IORQ}}))$$

It is very convenient that the common term is the function of the 25LS2521 8-bit comparator. Since this is ANDed with the remainder of the expression, we can use this to enable the 25LS2521. Thus

$$6850 \text{ enable} = (25LS2521 \text{ function}) \text{ \& } (25LS2521 \text{ enable}).$$

Finally, we note that *mode = mem* and *mode = port* are mutually exclusive as they are derived from the opposite settings of the same switch. This gives us our final logic diagram summarised in figure 5.6. As before, we do not use either CS0 or CS1 and so these have to be forced high by a pull-up resistor. Note that the eighth A/B pair on the comparator are grounded to ensure that they *always* match.

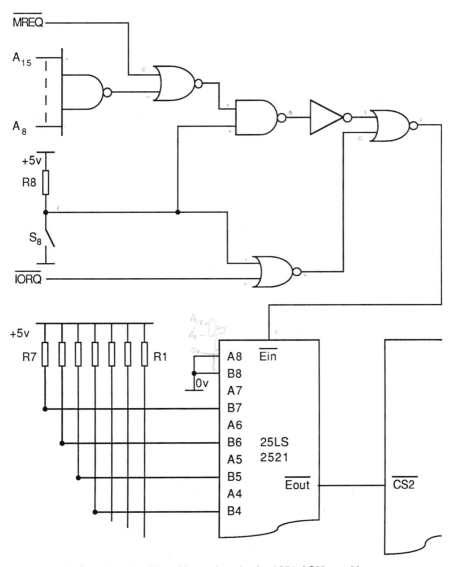

Figure 5.6 Switch selectable address decoder for 6850 ACIA as either a memory mapped or port input/output device

Chapter 6

Input/Output Programming

6.1 A Simple Device - The 6850 ACIA

Now that we have seen how a peripheral device is connected to the system, we can now move on to see how the device is programmed. We will start by considering a simple device like the 6850 Asynchronous Communications Interface Adaptor (ACIA). It has already been noted that this device appears as four registers at two addresses. At the first address, the *control* and *status* registers appear. The control register is accessed by writing to this address while the status register is accessed by reading this address. At the other address, the *transmit* and *receive* data registers appear. In the same way, the transmit data register is accessible by writing and the receive data register by reading. The following diagram will remind us of the structure. Reference to appendix C is necessary only if a more complete description is required.

	$R/\overline{W} = 0$	$R/\overline{W} = 1$
RS = 0	Control Register	Status Register
RS = 1	Transmit Data Register	Receive Data Register

Let us consider each register in turn.

The *control register* allows us to specify the way in which the two serial interfaces (one for transmit and one for receive) are to operate. For example, in serial transmission the rate at which data travels along the serial line is determined by the *Baud rate*. This has units of bits per second and is quite simply given by the time for which each bit in the transmission is valid or active. The Baud rate may, to some extent, be selected by program through the control register. We are able to select whether the clock that is supplied to the 6850 is to be divided by 1, 16 or 64 before being used as the transmit or receive clock. The data that is transmitted may be either seven or eight bits in length and may in the former case be checked by an optional parity bit. The way in which the data item is constructed may further be selected through the control register. The data bits are transmitted within a time frame bounded by start and stop bits. A start bit always lasts for as long as a data bit, but the stop bit may optionally be chosen to be either of the same duration as a data bit or to last twice as long. The selection of one or two stop bits is also made through the control register. The control register allows certain other options relating to the operation of the interface to be selected.

The *status register* contains bits that allow the program to find out what is happening within the interface. For example, a bit exists that informs the program that some data has arrived at the interface and is now ready for collection from the receive data register. This is the *RDRF* (Receive Data Register Full) bit. A second bit, the *TDRE* (Transmit Data Register Empty) bit tells the program that the interface has finished sending the previous character and is now ready to send another. Three bits in the status register are dedicated to informing the program of errors detected in the communication. For example, if the program has asked the 6850 to perform parity checking and the check fails, the parity error bit is set.

The *transmit data register* is used when the program wishes to send data. The act of placing data into this register starts off the transmission. In order to denote that a transmission is in progress, the TDRE bit is cleared.

The *receive data register* is where the interface places received data ready for collection by the program. As soon as a received item of data is placed into this register by the interface, the RDRF bit is set. This bit is cleared as soon as the first read of this register takes place to show that *fresh* data is no longer available.

Armed with this information, we can set about writing a pair of Z-80 subroutines that will handle the 6850. We can construct one, GETCHR, that receives a character and a second, PUTCHR, that transmits a character. Let us consider each of these in turn assuming that the 6850 is interfaced to the Z-80 as a memory-mapped device at location $FF02_{16}$.

6.1.1 A Character Receiver

Let us define this subroutine to return the received character in register B. It is not sufficient for us to simply read the receive data register and copy this to register B. There may not yet be a fresh character in the receive data register. Instead, we must check the satus register to see whether a character is available. It is the RDRF bit that tells us this and so we check to see if it is set. If it is not set, we will simply wait until it is. Thus:

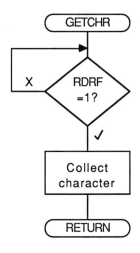

This may be translated into Z-80 assembly code in a number of ways - one is shown here:

```
GETCHR:   LD    HL,0FF02H   ;POINT TO ACIA STATUS REGISTER
GETCLP:   LD    A,(HL)      ;PICK UP STATUS REGISTER CONTENTS
          RRCA              ;SHIFT RDRF BIT INTO CARRY FLAG
          JR    NC,GETCLP   ;RDRF NOT SET - LOOP
          INC   HL          ;MOVE POINTER ON TO DATA REGISTER PAIR
          LD    B,(HL)      ;PICK UP RECEIVED CHARACTER
          RET               ;THEN RETURN
```

Note that the subroutine is implemented by means of a loop that simply waits for the RDRF bit to be set, just as shown in the flowchart. Note that if this were a generally available subroutine, we ought to have saved the registers that are used - specifically A, H and L - probably on the stack.

6.1.2 A Character Transmitter

This subroutine is defined to transmit the character passed in register B. It is essential that the ACIA be checked before sending to see that it is indeed ready to send a character. The TRDE bit in the status register conveys this information. We must therefore check this bit and wait for it to be set before sending the character, the latter operation being by simply placing the character into the transmit data register, thus:

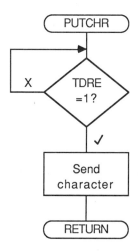

Turning this into Z-80 assembler, we might have:

```
PUTCHR:   LD    HL,0FF02H    ;POINT TO ACIA STATUS REGISTER
PUTCLP:   LD    A,(HL)       ;PICK UP STATUS REGISTER CONTENTS
          AND   2            ;LOOK AT TDRE BIT ONLY
          JR    Z,PUTCLP     ;TDRE NOT SET - LOOP
          INC   HL           ;MOVE POINTER ON TO DATA REGISTER PAIR
          LD    (HL),B       ;SEND CHARACTER
          RET                ;THEN RETURN
```

105

As with the character receiver, we see that we stay in a *wait loop*. This time, of course, we are waiting for the TDRE bit to be set. The same comments from above apply also to the question of making this a generally available subroutine.

6.1.3   Character Echoing

Often when a terminal (VDU) is connected to a computer system via a serial interface such as the 6850, it is configured so that what is typed upon the keyboard does not go *directly* to the screen. Only characters transmitted by the computer system are displayed. Thus, when a user types upon the keyboard, any characters that are supposed to be seen by the user have to be sent back or *echoed* to the screen. One resaon for this is that on many multi-access or time-sharing systems, the user has to supply a password as part of the logging-in procedure. This must not be allowed to show upon the screen and so is not echoed by the software running in the computer system.

Using the two subroutines that have already been written, we can construct a procedure, ECHO, that will receive *and echo* characters. This is simply done by calling the character receiver subroutine and then passing the received character to the character transmitter subroutine, thus:

```
ECHO:    CALL   GETCHR    ;COLLECT EACH CHARACTER AS IT ARRIVES
         CALL   PUTCHR    ;ECHO EACH CHARACTER
                :         ;ASSUME WE DO SOMETHING ...
                :         ;WITH EACH CHARACTER RECEIVED
         JP     ECHO      ;THEN DO IT ALL AGAIN
```

It is assumed in the above that we do in fact do something with the characters that are received and echoed. Typically, the characters would be placed into some sort of ordered, temporary storage area for later use as a complete, self-contained group of characters, for example, a line of text. This temporary storage area is referred to as a *buffer* area.

6.1.4 Character Buffering

The characters may be buffered in one of a number of different types of structure. The buffer may be a *linear* buffer where each slot in the buffer is effectively associated with a position upon the line of text that was received. This type of buffer might alternatively be referred to as a *line* buffer. An alternative, more common type of buffer is the *circular* buffer. Here, each newly received character is placed into the *next* available slot within the buffer as defined by a pointer, perhaps called the *fill* pointer. When the fill pointer reches the end of the buffer, it is made to point back to the top, thus making the buffer *circular.* Characters are removed from the buffer one by one according to another pointer - the *empty* pointer. Figure 6.1 shows this type of buffer with 6.1(a)

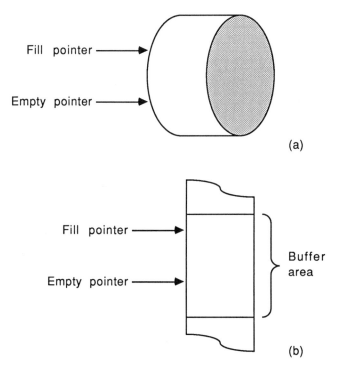

Figure 6.1 (a) Conceptual view and (b) Implementation of circular buffers

showing the conceptual view and 6.1(b) showing the implementation. Normally, the fill pointer will have a different value to the empty pointer, but occasionally they will be the same. This means that either the buffer is empty or it is full. How can we determine which it is? If the fill pointer has *caught up with* the empty pointer then the buffer is full but if the empty pointer has caught up with the fill pointer then the buffer is empty. Which pointer caught up with which is quite difficult to detect, so we introduce instead a count of the number of characters in the buffer. This is incremented every time a character is added to the buffer and decremented every time a character is removed. If the count is at zero then the buffer is empty and if it is at maximum then the buffer is full. Note that it is not *always* true to say that the count = fill pointer - empty pointer. In our example in figure 6.1(b), we see how the fill pointer has a value which is arithmetically less that that of the empty pointer. Instead, the count is always kept by incrementing and decrementing as characters are added to the buffer or removed from it. It is easy to consider how the state of a circular buffer would be maintained within a program. A *structure* could be set up that describes the current state of the buffer and how to initialise it. We would need to store within the structure the following information:

- the buffer count
- the fill pointer
- the empty pointer
- the buffer start address
- the buffer size

The final two intems of the structure are new to us, but are easily explained, their use being connected with making the buffer circular. The buffer start pointer is used in resetting either pointer when it reaches the end of the assigned buffer area. The buffer size is used to determine when to reset the pointer to the start of the area.

It is common to have two buffers associated with each serial interface. One of the buffers is used to store characters as they arrive and the other is used to buffer characters prior to their being output, with a structure describing each of them.

Rather than echoing the character by a direct call to the output subroutine PUTCHR as soon as the character arrives, it might be preferable to buffer the newly arrived character in the input buffer and to pass to the output buffer any characters that are to be echoed. The routine PUTCHR may then be called when characters exist within the output buffer. In order that we might be able to perform input and output simultaneously, we might choose to build up a sequence such as:

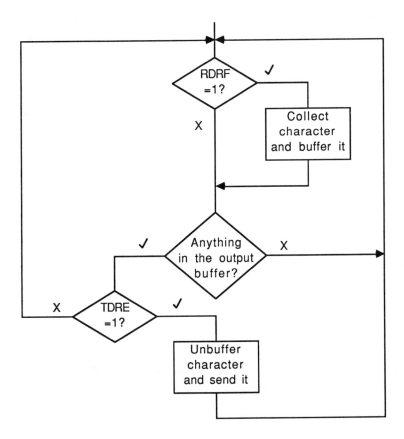

Any characters received are buffered in one or both of the buffers and any other characters required to be transmitted are placed in the output buffer. These are sent as and when the interface is ready. The sequence idles when RDRF is not set and there is nothing in the output buffer.

6.2 Doing More

If all that is required is that a system responds to typed (or otherwise supplied) input by processing it and producing output, then the scheme jst described is sufficient. It is more likely, though, that input and output from serial interfaces and other devices will form only part of what a computer system has to do. Some long term processing may need to be performed and it would be tedious to continually call the above sequence just in case some input has been received or some output has been placed into the output buffer.

Many computer systems are capable of serving more than one user at a time. In these *multi-access* systems, a large amount of time could be wasted checking to see if there is any input or output to do and this would be compounded by the fact that there are many terminals connected to the system. Indeed, it is hard to imagine how *any* useful work would be done by the system in such a situation. An alternative must be sought and this is available in the form of an *interrupt*. The question of interrupts is considered in the following chapter.

Another point that needs to be considered at this stage is whether the program is capable of taking in or sending out data at the rate that is required by the device. Many devices such as disks are capable of producing or accepting data at the rate of a number of characters per microsecond. We cannot contemplate our programs that we have shown above or even an interrupt driven program being able to take or supply data at this rate. An alternative must be found here too. The solution is to allow the device controller to have direct access to the memory. This technique of *direct memory access* is considered in chapter 8.

Chapter 7

Interrupt Structures

7.1 The Need for Interrupts

It has been noted in the previous chapter that there will be times when we cannot or would rather not afford to spend lots of time checking to see whether or not an interface has data available for us or is willing to despatch data for us. It would be much better if we could make use of a scheme whereby the interface in question informs the software that it has something for it or is ready to perform some function. For example, it would be desirable if the 6850 serial interface could in some way signal to the software when it has received a character on its input side or when it is ready to send a character on its output side. This signal comes from the device in the form of an *interrupt*.

7.2 The Effect of an Interrupt

If the software is informed by the interrupt mechanism that the interface has some data for it, to take one example, then the software should arrange to temporarily stop what it is doing and turn its attention instead to the device in question. Once the character or whatever has been collected from the device and at least buffered, the sequence that was taking place at the time of the interrupt can be resumed. This highlights two important features that the interrupt mechanism must possess. It must first have a means by which a section of program that is dedicated to handling the condition - the *interrupt service routine* - may be located. There may be a direct link to the handling software or there may be a slightly longer path. Secondly, before starting to run the software that is selected for this task, arrangements must be made for remembering the address to which to return to the interrupted sequence once the cause of the interrupt has been dealt with. Figure 7.1 shows entry to and return from an interrupt service routine. The latter requirement of arranging to return to an interrupted sequence is

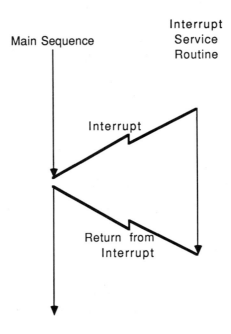

Figure 7.1 The topology of an interrupt

similar to something that is already familiar to us. We have seen in a subroutine CALL that the address of the subroutine is specified within the instruction and that the *return address* is placed on to the stack before the subroutine is entered. The same mechanism for storing the return address is, on the whole, used for interrupts. The requirement that the processor should be able to select a routine that will handle the cause of the interrupt is satisfied in one of a number of different ways, depending upon the processor in question.

Simple interrupt systems might have only one *entry point* for all interrupts. The routine that is entered from this must, in the case of multiple interrupt sources, decide which of the devices capable of generating interrupts did in fact do so. This process is known as *polling*, allowing the interrupt service routine to be located. Other systems are able to directly identify the interrupt service routine for a particular device. Such schemes exhibit *vectoring*. Both of these techniques will be investigated in what follows, but first we investigate some general hardware requirements connected with interrupt systems.

7.3 General Interrupt Sequences

7.3.1 Requesting an Interrupt

Any device wishing to raise an interrupt must signal this to the processor. This normally takes place by the device asserting some signal on the bus which ultimately arrives at the processor. This is generally referred to as the *interrupt request*. When a processor is designed, it is impossible to predict how many interrupt request inputs will be required in the biggest system based upon this processor. As a result, it is not usual for the processor to offer a number of interrupt request lines and for the devices to be connected to one each. Instead, the normal scheme is to have one (in most small processors) or some other small number (perhaps four in more sophisticated processors) of *common* request lines. Every device capable of requesting an interrupt does so along one of these lines. The requirement is that these potential requests from the devices on the common request line should be logically OR-ed together. This is done by the devices using rather special types of logic gates on their outputs to the common request line, namely *open-collector* gates.

7.3.1.1 Open-Collector gates

The output of a normal logic gate will assume one of two logic levels. It is constructed so that the output is always either low (with a voltage at almost 0) or high (with a voltage above about 2.5 volts). If we connect together two of these gates, and one is attempting to assert a high whilst the other is attempting to assert a low, the resulting logic level is difficult to predict, but the probable outcome is predictable - namely a damaged output. An open-collector gate output also has two states, but one of these is different from a normal logic gate. The two states of an open-collector gate are low (given by a voltage at almost 0) and floating (effectively no connection giving an undefined voltage). The floating state is assumed at the time when a normal logic gate would have a high output. The conceptual view of the outputs of a normal gate and an open-collector gate may be compared in the figure 7.2. In both types of gate we see an imaginary switch that may be in one of two positions - one for the logic '0' output and the other for the logic '1' output. In both cases, the logic '0' output causes the imaginary switch to move to the lower position and to pick up the normal logic '0' voltage level. It is the action taken for a logic '1' that differs. In the normal gate, the switch in the upper position picks up the normal logic '1' voltage. This may be thought

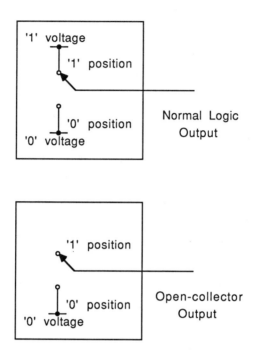

Figure 7.2 Conceptual view of normal and open-collector gates

of as being provided by a resistor (called a pull-up resistor) wired to the supply voltage. In the case of the open-collector gate, this resistor is missing. In fact, there is effectively no connection to the logic '1' switch position. Thus the voltage on the output pins *floats* to the voltage level on the line to which the output is connected.

Let us see what happens when open-collector devices are connected together on a common request line like an interrupt request line. In figure 7.3 (a), devices A and C are not requesting an interrupt and therefore have their outputs at logic '1' - floating. Device B, on the other hand, is attempting to request an interrupt by asserting a logic '0'. Since devices A and C effectively have their outputs disconnected from the request line, and device C is pulling the line down to a logic '0', the line resides at nearly 0 volts and the processor sees a logic '0'. In figure 7.3 (b), device A is also attempting to request. It also asserts a logic '0'. We now have two devices requesting and the third not. Devices A and B are both pulling the line down to a voltage near 0, but C effectively remains disconnected from the line. Still the processor sees a logic '0' and no devices are having their outputs stressed by conflicting voltage levels.

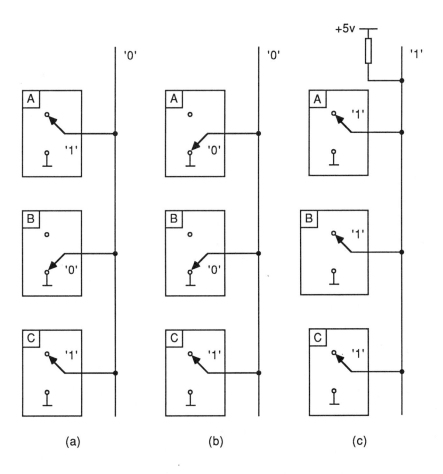

(a)　　　　　　　(b)　　　　　　　(c)

Figure 7.3 Three devices on the same common request line using open-collector outputs

Figure 7.3 (c) shows the situation when none of the devices are attempting to request. We note that none of the outputs are placing a voltage on the common request line - the whole line *floats*. In order that we can ensure that it *floats* to a logic '1', so that the processor knows that no device is requesting, we must pull the request line up with a resistor to the supply. If we choose a value of around 1K, we do not violate any of the rules about connecting logic outputs together since any output can *pull down* the line thus configured.

7.3.2   Identifying the Interrupting Device

It has already been noted that on some processors, the interrupt service routine for a given device can be selected directly. This usually involves the device in identifying itself to the processor upon some specific invitation from the processor. This invitation takes the form of an *interrupt acknowledge* signal from the processor. It is generated by the processor at a time when it is prepared to undertake the servicing of the interrupt according to the conditions laid down for such within the logic of the processor. We shall see more of what these conditions are later on. The device, in the general case, will identify itself by sending some unique bit pattern along the data lines in response to the acknowledge.

7.3.2.1   The Interrupt Acknowledge Signal

Having seen that more than one device can be on an interrupt request line, this raises a question about the interrupt acknowledge signal. In any system where there is only one common request line, there will also be only one acknowledge line. If there are four request lines, for example, there will probably be four acknowledge lines. In any case there is likely to be more than one device on any acknowledge line. If at any particular time, more than one device is requesting an interrupt, then it must be ensured that any acknowledge generated by the processor is seen by only *one* device. If more than one device were to see the signal, then the pattern on the data bus would be corrupted due to there being two devices driving data on to the data lines. Most bus lines are *bidirectional* . As such they relay information to or from all devices in parallel and at the same time. This is not acceptble for the interrupt acknowledge line. This line must be passed through each device in turn until a requesting device receives it and prevents it proceeding any further down the line. The type of line used to achieve this is known as a *unidirectional* line and the technique of passing the signal through each device until intercepted is known as *daisy-chaining*. Figure 7.4 shows this technique in action.

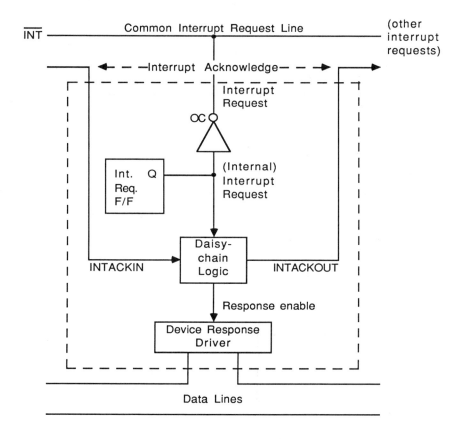

Figure 7.4 Daisy-chain operation

Each device in turn receives the acknowledge signal. In most cases it will have been passed to it from the device physically preceeding it. The device receiving the signal, which we shall now call Interrupt Acknowledge *In*, and decides whether or not to pass on the acknowledge to the next device in line (Interrupt Acknowledge *Out*) or to keep it. In the latter case the signal is used to (eventually) place on to the bus the device response that identifies it. The response may not be immediate but may have to be synchronised to some further timing signal from the processor. The operation of the

117

daisy-chain logic is expressed in the following truth table:

Device Interrupt Request	Interrupt Acknowledge In	Interrupt Acknowledge Out	Device Response Enable
0	0	0	0
0	1	1	0
1	0	0	0
1	1	0	1

The Device Interrupt Request is derived from an internal request which is held in some flip-flop - the Interrupt Request Flip-flop. This is set when the condition requiring attention occurs and is cleared as soon as the condition requiring attention is satisfied. It is from this flip-flop that the Interrupt Request to the processor is derived through an open-collector gate. We must not use the common interrupt request line for this logic, as it will be active whenever *any* device in the system requests an interrupt. Inspection of the truth table reveals that the Device Response Enable signal is simply the AND of

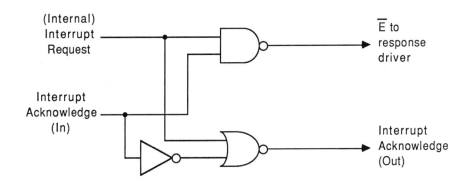

Figure 7.5 Daisy-chain Logic

the two inputs Device Interrupt Request and Interrupt Acknowledge In whist the Interrupt Acknowledge Out signal is given by Interrupt Acknowledge In AND not Interupt Request. The daisy-chain logic is as shown in figure 7.5.

7.4 Interrupts on the Z-80

There are two distinct types of interrupt on the Z-80, the *non-maskable* interrupt and the *maskable* interrupt.

7.4.1 Z-80 Non-Maskable Interrupts

The non-maskable interrupt cannot be ignored by the program, whereas the program can decide whether or not it wishes to see maskable interrupts. The non-maskable interrupt is requested by a device simply applying a negative-going pulse to the $\overline{\text{NMI}}$ pin of the processor. At the end of the current instruction cycle, the processor suspends its current action by stacking the PC and executing instead the instruction at location 66_{16}. An ISR to take care of the non-maskable interrupt is assumed to start at this location.

7.4.2 Z-80 Maskable Interrupts

Maskable interrupts may be turned on and off by program, using the *EI* (Enable Interrupts) and *DI* (Disable Interrupts) instructions, respectively. When interrupts are enabled, any request made via the $\overline{\text{INT}}$ pin will be allowed, but while interrupts are disabled, any request will be ignored. In the latter case, the device making the request will normally hold the request until it is seen by the processor. Interrupts are disabled automatically when the processor is RESET and also when an interrupt request is seen and acknowledged.

The action taken by the processor on seeing and allowing a maskable interrupt depends upon the current interrupt mode set for the processor. The Z-80 has three *modes* of maskable interrupt response - modes 0, 1 and 2. The current mode of interrupt response is set by the program by means of one of the three instructions:

```
IM   0          ;set interrupt mode 0
IM   1          ;set interrupt mode 1
IM   2          ;set interrupt mode 2
```

Mode 0 is the default mode which is adopted after a processor RESET. This is done to maintain compatability with the 8080 and 8085 processors which have only one mode of interrupt response which is identical to Z-80 mode 0. Since they have only one mode, they do not have the IM instructions.

7.4.2.1   Mode 1

This is the simplest of the modes. Upon allowing an interrupt, the processor stacks the PC and jumps to location 38_{16}. This interrupt mode is *non-vectored*. Hence, whatever the actual cause of the interrupt, the ISR residing at a memory location fixed by the hardware is executed. This influences the type of system for which this mode would be chosen, as will be discussed later.

7.4.2.2   Mode 0

When the processor allows an interrupt in mode 0, it first issues an interrupt acknowledge signal. Inspection of the Z-80 pin-out will reveal that there is no specific interrupt acknowledge pin. The acknowledgement is made by the processor asserting together the signals $\overline{M1}$ and $\overline{IORQ}$. The $\overline{M1}$ signal normally denotes that the processor is fetching the op-code part of an instruction (Machine cycle 1). $\overline{IORQ}$ normally indicates that the current bus cycle is accessing an Input/Output device (Input/Output ReQuest). The combination of these two signals would normally not occur, so they may be used to denote Interrupt Acknowledge. The interrupt acknowledge is actually an invitation to the device requesting the interrupt to identify itself so that the processor can select the correct ISR. The device does this by placing an 8-bit pattern on the data lines. This pattern is interpreted by the processor as an instruction. It is now that we can perhaps see the logic behind the choice of the rather odd combination of $\overline{M1}$ and $\overline{IORQ}$ for the acknowledge. $\overline{M1}$ and $\overline{IORQ}$ suggest "fetch an instruction from an input/output device" and this is exactly what happens.

Ultimately we wish to arrive at an interrupt service routine having remembered where we were interrupted. This is just like the action of a subroutine. We would, ideally like the device to supply a CALL (subroutine jump) instruction. This, however, is a 24-bit instruction made up of an 8-bit op-code and a 16-bit address. This would require the device to place three separate 8-bit patterns on to the bus, carefully sequenced and timed. Although the processor can cope with this and the device can be built to deal with this, it is over complicated. We look for a simpler solution.

The Z-80 has eight RESTART instructions. These are a set of 8-bit instructions that behave like CALL instructions but have a limited range. The RESTART instructions looks like

$$1\ 1\ X\ X\ X\ 1\ 1\ 1$$

where XXX determines the address to which the processor is to jump. Since XXX is three bits in length, there must be eight possible addresses to which the processor will jump. These addresses are given by XXX x 8. Thus, the pattern

$$1\ 1\ 0\ 1\ 0\ 1\ 1\ 1$$

will cause the processor to jump to location 16_{10} or 10_{16}. This is equivalent to CALL 10_{16}. Note that a program may use the RESTART instructions as software interrupts. In this case, the op-code is RST n, where n is the address to which the *call* takes place. In our example above, the instruction could be written as RST 10_{16}.

The execution of the RESTART instruction, then, causes the PC to be stacked and the program counter to be re-loaded with the address XXX x 8. Note that in this mode, it is the execution of the CALL or RESTART instruction provided by the device that causes the PC to be stacked. If any other instruction had been supplied by the device, no automatic stacking of the PC would take place. Instead, the instruction provided would be executed.

Note that RST 0 causes a jump to location 0 and so does placing a low on the $\overline{\text{RESET}}$ pin. Thus, it is likely that this location will have to be reserved for RESET rather than RST 0 and its notional interrupt source. This effectively limits the number of RESTART instructions available to the interrupt system to seven rather than eight.

In summary, then, the processor responds to the interrupt request with an interrupt acknowledge ($\overline{\text{M1}}$ & $\overline{\text{IORQ}}$). The device in turn responds to the interrupt acknowledge with an 8-bit pattern on the data lines which is interpreted by the processor as an instruction.

7.4.2.3 Mode 2

In this mode, the processor issues an acknowledge signal ($\overline{\text{M1}}$ & $\overline{\text{IORQ}}$ again) in response to the request. It expects an 8-bit pattern on the data lines in response to the acknowledge. This is exactly as in mode 0. However, in mode 2, the processor interprets the 8-bit pattern as part of an address. The complete address provides a means of selecting the correct ISR to service this interrupt. The 8-bit address supplied by the device is concatenated (joined end to end) with the contents of an 8-bit *Interrupt Register* (IR). The contents of this register is assumed to have been previously set up by the program by means of the LD I,A instruction. The resulting 16-bit address points to an entry in a table of ISR addresses. Since an ISR address is 16 bits in length, each entry in the table will take up two words. The table is assumed to contain, therefore, pairs of words that each give the address of an ISR, with the least significant half of the address being in the position in the table given by the lower, even address. In order to ensure that the table is of the correct format, namely that each *even + next odd* pair contains a 16-bit address, the least significant bit of the pattern supplied by the device must be zero. The diagram in figure 7.6 explains the process.

It can be seen that since we have an eight bit pattern from the device (combined with the contents of a processor register) effectively pointing to word-pairs in a table, then we have the ability to select one of 128 word-pairs or ISR addresses. Thus the pattern from the device can uniquely select one of 128 different ISR entry points. This is an example of a *vectored* interrupt system.

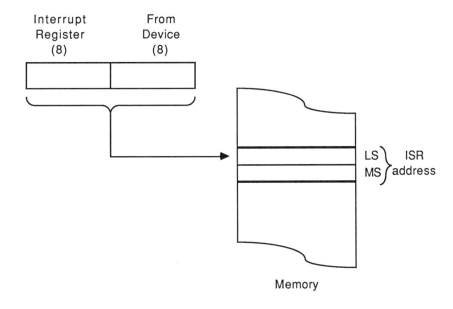

Figure 7.6 Z-80 Mode 2 interrupt operation

Now a word about the Interrupt Register. The contents of this register may, as has been stated, be set by the program. The contents of this register, if concatenated with eight zeros, may be thought of as pointing to the *start* of a table of 128 ISR addresses (each of two words). We might call this table the *Interrupt Vector Table*. The pattern from the device is simply, then, an index into this table, the position of which is defined by the contents of the Interrupt Register. From this, we can see that it is possible for the program to move around from one table of ISR addresses to another as the system runs, thus giving the ability to change the precise interrupt response to any one or more devices even if the tables are in PROM.

7.4.3   Interrupt Scheme Choices

The flexibility of the Z-80 interrupt scheme allows a degree of choice in design of hardware and software. These choices are now discussed.

7.4.3.1   Non-Maskable vs Maskable Interrupts

In normal use, we would tend to reserve the non-maskable interrupt input for devices that warn of some major fault. For example, if we have a device that warns of power supply failure, then we would connect that to the $\overline{\text{NMI}}$ input so that the program would get to know of the power failure as soon as possible in case it needs to save vital data. Interrupts from what might be called "normal" sources like peripheral devices, would be connected via the $\overline{\text{INT}}$ line so that the program has the option of ignoring them.

7.4.3.2   Factors Influencing the Choice of Mode

The interrupt mode chosen for a particular system depends primarily on the number of interrupt sources in the system. If we have a system with only a single interrupt source, then mode 1 would be the obvious choice. This is because no additional logic is required to handle the interrupt acknowledge, since the processor is not expecting any response from the device in this mode. When more than one device is to be place in the interrupt system, the choice of mode 0 or mode 2 is a little more open. In both modes, the device will require the additional logic necessary to allow it to respond to the interrupt acknowledge and so the choice of mode cannot be based on the hardware requirement alone. Instead, we must consider the two schemes purely from the software point of view. Mode 0 allows up to seven interrupt sources to be connected without losing the uniqueness of selection of the ISR. (Remember that it is seven and not eight since location 0 is used when a processor RESET is issued). If we have more than seven interrupt sources then mode 2 is probably the choice, but if we have seven or fewer, then the flexibility of mode 2 against mode 0 must be considered, although it must be remembered that mode 2 requires slightly more memory due to the *indirect* nature of the location of the ISRs.

7.4.4 Enabling and Disabling Interrupts

We have already seen that interrupts can be enabled or disabled by the instructions EI and DI respectively. No matter which interrupt mode the processor is in and no matter what pattern the device sends in, maskable interrupts are automatically disabled when the interrupt is allowed by the processor. The current state of maskable interrupt enable/disable is noted in the processor's internal *Interrupt Enable Flip-Flop* (IEFF). This is cleared when an interrupt is allowed to denote that interrupts are no longer enabled. If we wish to go on seeing interrupts, we must re-enable interrupts (using EI). This is usually done at some time before leaving the ISR.

On acceptance of a non-maskable interrupt, the IEFF is cleared to disable any maskable interrupts that might occur during the servicing of the non-maskable interrupt. At the end of the non-maskable ISR, we would normally wish to reinstate the maskable interrupt enable/disable state as reflected by the IEFF. However, the non-maskable ISR has no idea of the state of the IEFF immediately prior to entry to the non-maskable interrupt and so cannot simply execute an EI or not as the case may be. Here we need some hardware assistance. Quite simply, the processor employs a second flip-flop (IEFF2) that acts as a background copy of the main flip-flop (now renamed IEFF1) upon entry to the non-maskable ISR. So, on recognition of a non-maskable interrupt, the processor copies IEFF1 to IEFF2 and then clears IEFF1, thus disabling maskable interrupts. At the end of the non-maskable ISR, the execution of an *RETN* (RETurn from Non-maskable interrupt) instruction causes the contents of the background flip-flop (IEFF2) to be copied back into the main one (IEFF1) before unstacking the former value of the program counter.

The action of the two interrupt enable flip-flops in all cases in which either is affected is detailed in the table below.

125

Action	IEFF1	IEFF2	Comments
CPU RESET	0	0	Maskable interrupt disabled
DI instruction execution	0	0	Maskable interrupt disabled
EI instruction execution	1	1	Maskable interrupt enabled
Accept NMI	0	IEFF1	IEFF1->IEFF2 Maskable interrupt disabled
RETN instruction execution	IEFF2	-	IEFF2 -> IEFF1 at completion of $\overline{NMI}$ service routine

Note that the return from maskable interrupt (RETI) instruction has no effect on either of the two interrupt enable flip-flops. As has been stated, if it is required that further interrupts are to be sought after completion of this ISR, interrupts must be specifically re-enabled by use of the EI instruction at some time before the end of the ISR. It is worthy of note here that the EI instruction does not have an immediate effect. The setting of the interrupt enable flip-flops takes place at the completion of the instruction following the EI instruction thus guaranteeing that if the ISR ends

```
EI
RETI
```

The program sequence will actually leave this ISR even if it is dragged straight back into another. If this were not the case, the stack would soon overflow.

7.5   What Does an Interrupt Service Routine (ISR) Do?

The main task of an Interrupt Service Routine is to take care of the cause of the interrupt. If it fails to do this, it is highly likely that the device will maintain its interrupt request and the program will be interrupted again. For example, if the device has raised an interrupt because data is available (its DONE bit is set) and the ISR fails to take that data from the device, then the DONE bit will remain set and the interrupt request will remain. Remember that it is the presence of the DONE bit that (ultimately) generates the interrupt request. Since the process of servicing an interrupt will probably make use of the processor registers, we must save those that we use so that the interrupted program is unaware that an interrupt has occurred. The state of the registers must be restored before returning from the interrupt.

If the interrupt is a maskable interrupt and presumably therefore nothing special, then we will need to re-enable interrupts before returning.

7.6 Interrupts on the UNIBUS (PDP-11)

7.6.1 Hardware Aspects

There are four interrupt request lines (BR4, BR5, BR6 and BR7) and four interrupt acknowledge lines (BG4, BG5, BG6 and BG7) on the UNIBUS. *BR* stands for Bus Request and *BG* stands for Bus Grant. The names bus request and bus grant give a clue to the process by which a device requests an interrupt. Any device wishing to request an interrupt must first become *bus master*. It attempts to do this by asserting one of the bus request signals. In theory, the fact that a device has asserted its BR line does not necessarily mean that it is going to request an interupt, although usually the BR lines are used only for interrupt requests.

The bus request lines are organised on a priority basis with BR7 as the highest priority. Any particular device requests only on one BR line and inspects the equivalent BG line for the acknowledge. The BR/BG combination for any device may be changed only at the hardware level - by means of a soldering iron or a special plug on the device interface board. We will call this the *hardware priority level* of the device.

The processor also has a priority level. The current processor priority level is retained by the processor in three bits of the Processor Status Word (PSW). In addition to being an internal processor register, this is a memory mapped register that occupies the highest memory address and as such is also available to the program. As a matter of interest, the least significant five bits of this register constitute the PDP-11's flag register as shown in figure 7.7. The use of the remaining eight bits of this register do not concern us directly here and indeed varies from one model of PDP-11 to the next. Unlike that of devices, the processor priority level is variable. It may be changed by program, as we have already shown and also by the hardware of the interrupt system.

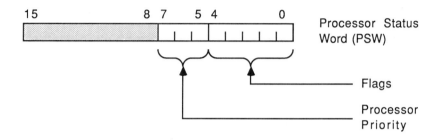

Figure 7.7 PDP-11 Processor Status Word (PSW)

At the end of each *instruction* cycle, the processor samples the BR lines starting with BR7 and proceeding in priority order until it finds a request (or not). Thus, if a request exists on both BR6 and BR4, the one on BR6 is noted and the scan stops. The request on BR4 is not seen at this stage. If a request is found, its priority level (given by the BR line on which it is made) is compared with the current processor priority held in the processor status word. The interrupt is allowed only if the priority level of the request is strictly *greater* than the current processor priority level. Thus, if the processor priority level is currently at 5, requests from devices with priority levels of 4 or 5 are ignored and those from devices at levels 6 and 7 are seen. We could view this as interrupts from levels 4 and 5 being disabled and those from levels 6 and 7 being enabled. This implies that setting the processor priority level at 7 disables all interrupts whilst setting it at any level between 0 and 3 enables all interrupts.

The diagram in figure 7.8 shows how the priority level of the processor influences the devices for which interrupts are enabled. For a given processor priority level, devices assigned to any BR level above the line representing the processor priority have their interrupts enabled whilst those below the line have their interrupts disabled. For example, if the processor is running at priority level 5 as shown, then requests from devices on levels 4 and 5 will be disabled, whilst those from devices on levels 6 and 7 will be enabled. It can clearly be seen that processor priority levels 0 - 3 are essentially the same in that all three allow interrupts from all devices. Further, setting the processor at priority level 7 has the effect of disabling all device interrupts.

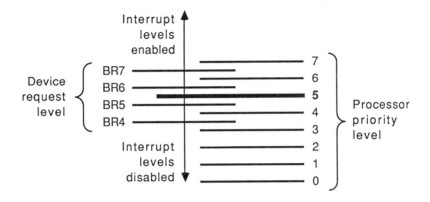

Figure 7.8 Relationship between device and processor priority levels

Having decided to accept a particular interrupt, the processor acknowledges it by asserting the appropriate BG signal. This is daisy-chained through all devices occupying that level eventually to find the first device requesting an interrupt on that level. The bus grant is prevented, by this device, from passing any further down the bus. The selected device has now achieved bus mastership - the necessary prelude to requesting an interrupt. The device marks its selection by asserting *SACK* (Selection ACKnowledge). At this point, BR is no longer required since the interrupting device has achieved bus mastership. Thus the BR is now removed by the device, in response to which BG is removed by the processor. The bus control logic monitors the bus to ensure that a SACK signal is produced in response to the BG. If no response is detected within 5 to 10 microseconds (depending upon model of processor), the BG is removed and the system continues as though there had been no BR. A second signal *BBSY* (Bus BuSY) is asserted to inform other devices that bus mastership has been assumed by the selected device. The device actually becomes bus master at the time of the assertion of BBSY.

The device now starts the process of identifying itself by placing a bit pattern on the data lines. Once the data is on the data lines, the device asserts the *INTR* (INTerrupt Request) signal. This signal serves a dual purpose. It acts firstly as a signal to denote that the device is in fact requesting an interrupt and secondly as a timing signal, very much like MSYN. Once INTR has been asserted, SACK may be removed. The fact that an interrupt is requested means that the processor is the slave and as such it takes the data from the data lines after a short delay for the data to settle. The processor informs the device that it has taken the data from the data lines by asserting SSYN just as if this were a normal bus transaction. In response to the SSYN, the interrupting device removes the data, INTR and BBSY.

The processor now has a data pattern that identifies the interrupting device. This pattern actually gives the address of the so called *interrupt vector* or *trap vector* for the selected device. A trap vector is a two word area, usually within the first 256 words of memory, that contains the following:

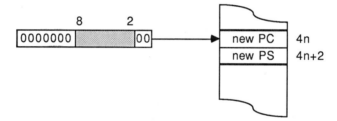

Although all sixteen bits are provided by the device, it is normal for only bits 8 - 2 (shaded in the diagram) to contain the device identification. Bits 15 - 9 are set to zero to limit the amount of space in memory that has to be dedicated to trap vectors whilst bits 1 and 0 are set to zero to ensure that the first word of the trap vector falls on a multiple of 4 (byte) address boundary. Within the trap vector thus defined, the *new PC* is, of course, the address of the ISR and is used to replace the PC once this has been stacked. The *new PS* is the processor status word to be adopted at the start of the ISR, having stacked the former PS. The implication of replacing the processor status word with one that is related to each interrupt is that we can instantly change the arrangement of the enabled and disabled devices - refer again to figure 7.8.

The next few cycles seen on the bus thus involve the stacking of the former PC and PS and the fetching of the new PC and PS from the specified interrupt vector.

7.6.2 Software Aspects

We have seen that when the device finally interrupts, it sends to the processor the address of the interrupt vector from which the processor both locates the interrupt service routine and sets the processor priority level. This new priority level, as we have seen, potentially alters the arrangement of the enabled and disabled devices. It is tempting to assume that *any* interrupt service routine should run at level 7, thus disabling *all* further interrupts, only to restore the level to somewhere between 0 and 3 immediately before returning to the interrupted sequence. This would completely duplicate the action of the Z-80 non-maskable interrupt scheme, but would be very inflexible. If we could write each interrupt service routine so that it can tolerate being interrupted, the situation could be improved. We could envisage a scheme whereby the priority level at which each interrupt service routine is run is in some way related to the hardware priority of the device. We could, for example, set the new processor priority level to the same value as the hardware level of the interrupting device. This would have the effect of disabling further interrupts from devices on the same and lower levels as the interrupting device whilst enabling those from higher priority devices. As long as we can have some confidence in the assignment of devices to levels, this would seem like a reasonable scheme. Another alternative is to set the processor priority level in the new PS to level 7 to disable all interrupts at the start of the interrupt service routine and to allow the interrupt service routine to reduce the level a little at a time as the interrupt service tasks become less time critical. We must remind ourselves at this stage that the processor priority level in the new PS entry in the interrupt vector is alterable by program, but that the hardware level on which the device interrupts is set in the hardware.

Note that on completion of the interrupt service routine, we must arrange for the stacked PC and PS to be returned to the processor PC and PS. The RTI instruction does this.

7.7 Device Interrupt Enabling and Disabling

We have seen how it is possible in the Z-80 to turn all interrupts on and off and how it is possible in the PDP-11 to turn groups of interrupts on and off. It is often necessary, though, to be able to turn off interrupts from one or two devices whilst maintaining interrupts from others. This could be done on the PDP-11 by careful assignment of devices to hardware priority levels, but it is unlikely that this would be satisfactory for all time. In the Z-80, this would not be possible. Thus we seek some other way of turning individual device interrupts on and off selectively. Each device should exhibit one or more *interrupt enable bits* that allow the program to control whether or not it wishes to receive interrupts from that device. In the 6850 ACIA, bit 7 of the control register controls the interrupt generation logic associated with the receiver. If this bit is set then the 6850 will generate an interrupt request when the RDRF bit is set to denote that a character has been received. If this bit is clear then the 6850 will not generate an interrupt under this condition. If this bit is newly set whilst RDRF is set, then an interrupt request will be generated immediately. There is a similar bit controlling transmitter interrupts. It would seem that the 6850 has some logic within it much like that of figure 7.9 in which the global interrupt request flag (reflected in bit 7 of the status register) is set if either the RDRF bit is set together with receiver interrupt enable or the TDRE bit is set together with the transmitter interrupt enable. Note the implication of the latter part

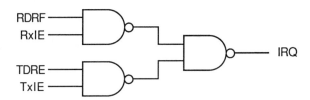

Figure 7.9 Equivalent interrupt logic of the 6850 ACIA

of the above statement when it is the case that the transmitter is ready to transmit (TDRE is set) whenever the transmitter is idle. If the program has been outputting characters from a buffer and the buffer has become empty then it will have finished transmitting for a while. It cannot simply treat the interrupt resulting from the final character output as if it had not occurred. If it did so, the program would be interrupted again and again for as long as TRDE remained set and the transmitter interrupt enable was set. The program must thus turn off transmitter interrupts whenever it has no more characters to output.

It is worth mentioning here that on an integrated system like the PDP-11 or any other processor using the UNIBUS, it is likely that the interrupt enable bits for each device will be in a standard position in the respective control registers. In fact, within UNIBUS devices, the interrupt enable bit is always bit 6.

7.8 Interrupt Programming

Taking into account what we now know of the hardware and software aspects of interrupt structures and of input/output device programming, we can turn our attention to constructing an interrupt driven program.

Appendix D contains an assembly listing of a Z-80 program to handle interrupts from a 6850 ACIA. The 6850 is defined as a memory-mapped device at locations $FF02_{16}$ and $FF03_{16}$. The program accepts characters from the keyboard by the use of interrupts and buffers and echoes them up to and including a carriage-return character. It then re-transmits the entire buffer back to the screen. The output is also under the control of interrupts.

Extensive comments within the listing serve to illustrate the action of the program.

Chapter 8

Direct Memory Access

8.1 Introduction

Many devices can produce or demand data so rapidly and in their own time that a programmed loop to gather the data cannot or should not be used. A programmed loop cannot be used if it cannot keep up with the demands of the device for speed. The devices produce or demand data at specific times and in many cases, if the data is not dealt with within a certain time, data will be lost. This is because most of the faster devices are rotating devices of some sort that cannot wait for data to be taken or provided. It could be that using a programmed loop to take data from or provide data to a device would be fast enough but would take up so much processor time that there would be very little left for running programs.

In either situation, we arrange for the device to gain direct access to the memory in order to transfer one or more words of data. This technique is known as *direct memory access* (DMA). The device gains access to the memory, for either reading or writing, without the intervention of the processor. The device must be equipped with a *device controller* capable of performing DMA. This controller in fact contains a hardware version of the programmed loop. The controller is primed with information defining the transfer and it then performs the transfer on its own whilst the processor continues with normal processing. When the transfer is complete, the controller sets a bit to convey this information. This bit may go on to produce an interrupt request, if the interrupt enable bit is set in the controller, in just the same way as a non-DMA or *character by character* device would.

In order to be able to transfer a word to the memory, the device performing DMA must first gain control of the bus, that is become bus master. It requests bus mastership from the processor and when this is granted it goes ahead and performs the transfer. Bus mastership may be granted to a device at the end of any *bus* cycle. The processor does not have to wait for the end of the instrction cycle before it can allow DMA since the program is not suspended in favour of another piece of program as in an interrupt. In order for the DMA transfer to take place, the program is merely prevented, for a short time, from making accesses to the memory. This will eventually have the probable effect of causing the program to have to wait since the processor cannot get to the memory precisely when it wishes to. We can thus appreciate the alternative term for DMA, namely *cycle stealing*.

8.2 The Program's View of DMA

To the program, direct memory access devices appear to perform transfers of whole blocks of data to or from the memory. The program that requests the transfer has to provide information that defines the transfer. The actual information that is sent to the controler depends on the type of device. If we consider a transfer from a disk, at least the following must be specified:

disk address	-	where on that drive
memory address	-	destination in memory
item (word/character) count	-	how much to transfer
direction of transfer	-	which way (READ in this case).

This may be generalised to:

source location for transfer
destination location for transfer
length of transfer
direction of transfer.

Once the transfer has been started, the program will, as has already been mentioned, either wait for some sort of DONE bit to appear or, more likely, return to some other task whilst awaiting an interrupt to mark the end of the transfer.

We will return to look at specific examples of transfers, but first we must examine the hardware aspects of DMA transfers.

8.3 Hardware Aspects of DMA

Once the DMA controller has been told exactly what to do by the program, it will go ahead and organise the transfer. There are two levels at which this occurs. The highest level is common to all DMA-equipped devices and concerns how the complete block of data is transferred between the device and memory. The lower level is processor dependent and is concerned with how the device gains bus mastership.

8.3.1 DMA Device Controller Operation - Satisfying the Program

The program passes to the device controller information that defines the transfer. It is up to the controller to satisfy this transfer request before reporting completion to the program. It has already been noted that the operation of the controller at this level duplicates the operation of the programmed loop but in hardware. It is in fact more than this, in that it further duplicates the operation of a program that transfers data from the device to a buffer in memory or *vice versa*. It is easy to imagine how this would be in program terms. For input, each data item would be received when ready and placed into the buffer at the next available point. For output, the opposite would occur. Each data item would be taken from the buffer and sent to the device when it is ready to deal with it. The preceding has, more or less, described the high level operation of the generalised DMA controller. Taking data input as an example, we may express the operation of the controller at this level in pseudo-Pascal as follows:

```
while item-count > 0 do
begin get-next-item-from-device;
      send-to-memory;
      bump-device-address;
      memory-address := memory-address + 1;
      item-count := item-count - 1
end;
set-done-bit;
```

The intended actions of the procedures that have been used but not declared should be fairly obvious. Of course, the way in which progress is made from one data item on the device to the next will depend almost entirely upon device structure. This is the reason for expressing this action as *bump-device-address* rather than simply *device-address := device-address + 1*. It is obvious that this is an oversimplification of the situation. For example, it has been assumed that the direction of transfer has been established and that this piece of *program* has been selected to satisfy that transfer request. However, it serves as an indication that it is possible to envisage the operation of the DMA controller as a piece of program implemented in hardware.

8.3.2 DMA Device Controller Operation - Interaction with the Bus

This is the part of the operation of the DMA controller that is processor dependent. In general, the device controller will request bus mastership and once this has been obtained will transfer one or more data items. The device must not occupy the bus for extended periods as there may be devices in the system that need more frequent access to the bus than this would allow. We must insist that a device does not gain control of the bus and then transfer a large block of data. Certainly the controller must not be allowed to complete the whole of a large transfer request, such as would be the case with a disk transfer, within one DMA request. If the controller has a buffer, it might be efficient for the device to save up eight or so data items and then to transfer them in a single burst of DMA activity within one DMA request.

Having established the ground-rules for DMA controller operation, it is now possible to go on to look at specific DMA schemes. As usual, we will look at each of the Z-80 and UNIBUS DMA schemes, bearing in mind that the Z-80 utilises a synchronous bus and the UNIBUS is asynchronous in nature.

8.3.2.1 DMA on the Z-80

A device wishing to make a direct access to memory must first request the use of the bus. Once it is established as bus master it performs a transfer in the normal way, asserting all of the normal address, control and, in the case of a write operation, data lines. A request for bus mastership is made by the device asserting the $\overline{\text{BUSRQ}}$ (BUS

ReQuest) line. This is implemented on the bus as a common request line and so all devices that might wish to make a request for bus mastership are connected to this one line by means of open-collector logic gates, as with the common interrupt request line. At the end of each *bus* cycle, the processor samples the $\overline{BUSRQ}$ line to see if any devices are currently requesting bus mastership. If this line is low, the processor replies with $\overline{BUSAK}$ (BUS AcKnowledge). This signal, which the processor uses to denote that it is willing to relinquish the bus, is daisy-chained through all devices that are capable of making a bus mastership request. The daisy-chain is established, as with the interrupt acknowledge scheme, to ensure that only one device gains bus mastership in the case that more than one device is requesting. When the processor asserts $\overline{BUSAK}$, it *disconnects* itself from the lines used for normal bus transactions - address, data, $\overline{RD}$, $\overline{WR}$, $\overline{MREQ}$, etc. This is possible since the processor is connected to these lines by means of *tri-state* outputs (see section 4.5.1.1). The processor simply sets its connections to these lines into the *high-impedance* state. Of course, since all devices that are capable of DMA transfers are also connected to these lines, they must in turn be capable of disconnecting themselves when they are not bus master. They must also, therefore, be connected to these lines through tri-state outputs.

Eventually the $\overline{BUSAK}$ signal reaches the requesting device. This device intercepts the signal thus preventing any devices further down the line from seeing the acknowledge. Once the $\overline{BUSAK}$ has been received, the requesting device is deemed to be bus master and may perform the transfer as any other bus master would by using all of the normal bus lines. If it wishes to transfer a word of data to memory location 1234, it simply places 1234 on to the address lines, the data to be written on to the data lines and then asserts $\overline{MREQ}$ and $\overline{WR}$ exactly as we saw in Chapter 3. When the transfer has been completed, the device controller removes the address, data, $\overline{MREQ}$ and $\overline{WR}$ signals and then signals to the processor that it has completed its transfer by also removing $\overline{BUSRQ}$. The processor then removes $\overline{BUSAK}$ and proceeds with the next bus cycle - unless, of course, a $\overline{BUSRQ}$ is outstanding from another device. In this case, the processor would not see the removal of $\overline{BUSRQ}$ and would simply assume that the same device still had the bus. The acknowledge would be given up by the device that had just finished its transfer and would be passed on to the next requesting device in sequence.

8.3.2.2 DMA on the UNIBUS

What follows is a slight simplification of the operation of DMA on the UNIBUS. The simplification is in the area of interlocking DMA requests from more than one device at a time. The bus controller has to satisfy itself that the request that it is seeing is new and genuine and not from the device that it has just allowed to use the bus. It does this by ensuring that certain signals have been inactive for certain times before allowing other events to occur. The detail of this only serves to cloud the true operation of the scheme and so is omitted for the sake of clarity.

As with any DMA scheme, the device controller wishing to perform a DMA transfer must first obtain bus mastership. On the UNIBUS, bus mastership is requested by the assertion of *NPR* (Non-Processor Request). This is a common request line and is therefore driven by an open-collector output. On completion of the current bus cycle, the bus controller senses the NPR and responds with *NPG* (Non-Processor Grant). This signal is daisy-chained through all interested devices and the first requesting device to receive the grant intercepts it. This device responds to the acknowledge with *SACK* (Selection ACKnowledge) and if only a single item of data is to be transferred (the normal situation in most cases) it removes NPR. The assertion of SACK is timed out by the bus controller after 5 - 10 microseconds depending upon the processor in use. This avoids the system hanging if a spurious NPG is received for some reason. The bus controller, upon receipt of SACK removes NPG. Having seen NPG removed, the device asserts *BBSY* (Bus BuSY) to confirm that it is now bus master. The newly assigned bus master now may use all of the normal bus signals to perform the required transfer. SACK may be removed at any time after BBSY is asserted. At the end of the transfer, the device controller removes BBSY (SACK must be removed before this) to mark that it has released the bus. The bus controller will now either give the bus to any other requesting device controller or give it back to the processor. The processor is the lowest in the priority list of units able to use the bus.

A great deal of similarity exists between DMA operation and interrupt operation on the UNIBUS. The reader is encouraged to investigate this. In both cases, it is possible to see the handshaking that goes on between the bus controller and the requesting device.

8.4 Programming DMA Devices

Many devices that utilise direct memory access are quite complex. It is the intention of this section to provide some insight into DMA device programming but without masking the concepts with unnecessary complexities. In order that a real device might be used as the basis of the description, a simple device and its controller is chosen. The device in question is the RK-05 disk sub-system that interfaces to the UNIBUS. This comprises a controller capable of supporting up to eight disk drives each handling a 2.4Mbyte exchangeable disk. Each disk has the following format:

Surfaces/drive: 2

Tracks/surface: 203

Sectors/track: 12

Bytes/sector: 512

The controller appears to the program as six registers. Some of these registers are read only whilst others are read/write. The registers and their mnemonic names are:

Control and Status (RKCS) read/write

Disk Address (RKDA) read/write

Current Bus Address (RKBA) read/write

Word Count (RKWC) read/write

Error (RKER) read only

Drive Status (RKDS) read only

Note that unlike the 6850 ACIA in which the control and status registers are separate and are write only and read only respectively, the RK05 has a single register for both control and status bits. Some of the bits in this register are read only, others are write only and the remainder are read/write. We will now examine the parts of these registers which are of interest by following how a typical transfer might be programmed. As each register is introduced, it will be shown diagramatically. Where a given bit is shaded, the bit in question is unused. Where a bit is not shaded but is at the same time not labelled, the bit in question is used in the interface but is of no interest in this discussion.

Before the program can request a transfer to be performed by the controller, it must ensure that the controller is not busy. As with other devices that we have seen, this controller has a DONE bit. This is in the *control and status* register (RKCS) and is known in this case as *controller ready*, as shown below:

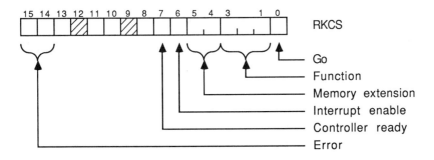

It is worth noting that the controller ready bit is bit 7. In a sixteen bit word made up of two eight bit bytes, bit 7 is the most significant bit of the least significant byte. The PDP-11 processor is capable of addressing bytes individually and therefore bit 7 is a very convenient position in which to place this DONE bit as it is easily testable with a sequence such as the following:

```
LOOP:  TSTB   RKCS      ;LOOK AT STATUS REGISTER
       BPL    LOOP      ;READY NOT SET - LOOP
```

The TSTB instruction looks at the byte addressed and summarises the contents in the flags. The BPL instruction causes a jump if the flags reveal that the contents of the lower byte of RKCS represent a positive quantity - that is if the sign bit (bit 7) is not set. Once it has been established that the controller is ready to receive the transfer request, the program can proceed to send the parameters that define the transfer. The order in which these are sent is of no significance since in this particular controller setting the GO bit (bit 0; RKCS) constitutes the signal that informs the controller that all parameters have been sent and that the transfer may now begin.

It will be assumed that the program is to request a read from disk into memory. This means that in terms of our general transfer parameters of section 8.2 the following conditions hold. The source of the transfer is the disk and the destination is memory. Hence the source location for the transfer is specified as a disk address and the destination location is specified as a memory address. The length of transfer is quite simply how many bytes are to transferred and the direction of transfer is specified as READ.

The program defines the disk address by use of the *disk address* register (RKDA), shown below:

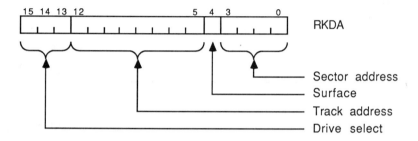

The program may select any one of the eight drives that the controller is capable of handling by means of the most significant three bits. The remaining bits specify the location of the start of the data on the selected drive. This is in terms of track, surface and sector addresses.

The memory address is now specified in the *current bus address* register (RKBA). This is simply a sixteen bit register that contains the current bus (usually memory) address. Remembering that the UNIBUS has eighteen address lines, it is clear that there must be a method for specifying the remaining two bits of the address. Reference back to RKCS reveals the answer. Bits 5 and 4 are labelled *memory extension* and it is these bits that effectively contain A_{17} and A_{16}, respectively. Hence, setting the memory address is a case of making a write to RKBA with bits 15 - 0 and to RKCS with bits 17 and 16.

The amount of data to be transferred is specified in the *word count* register (RKWC). This is defined to contain the 2's complement of the number of words to be transferred. The 2's complement is used so that the controller can increment this register after each word (2 bytes) has been transferred, stopping when it reaches zero. It is easier to increment in hardware than it is to decrement. Since RKWC is a 16-bit register, the maximum amount of data that can be transferred at one time is 64K words or 128K bytes. Note that placing zero into this register will cause 64K words to be transferred as the word count in this register is decremented before it is tested for zero. It is, of course, possible to specify a word count that is not a multiple of 256 (the number of words per sector). In this case, the whole sector is read by the controller so that the necessary data integrity checks may be performed, but only the requested amount of data is actually transferred to the memory. In the case of a write, the controller will write the whole sector. It is therefore not possible to change the first *n* words of a sector without reading in the sector and changing it in memory before writing it back again.

All that remains to be specified now is the direction of the transfer. Reference again to RKCS reveals that there are three bits (bits 2 - 0) reserved for *function*. These allow up to eight functions or operations to be specified on the drive selected by the address in RKDA. The functions available are:

000 Controller RESET
001 Write (to disk)
010 Read (from disk)
011 Write check (verify data just written)
100 Seek (locate track, surface and sector; no data transferred)
101 Read check (verify data just read)
110 Drive RESET
111 Write lock (set drive write protection)

The function that we require in this case is 010 and this is placed in bits 2 - 0 of RKCS.

When all of the parameters defining the transfer have been sent, the GO bit (bit 0; RKCS) may be set. This, rather unusually, is a nominally write only bit in that when the program sets this bit and then attempts to read it back again, it will always read back as 0. The controller will clear the DONE bit to denote that it is busy and then go on to perform the selected function, setting the DONE bit again once the operation is complete. As with any other interface, the setting of the done bit by the hardware may be detected in the program by either a programmed loop or by the use of the interrupt system. The latter comes into play when the interrupt enable bit (bit 6; RKCS) is set. If any problems occurred during the operation, one or both of the ERROR bits in RKCS will be set, together with the appropriate bit(s) in the *error* register (RKER). The definitions of some of the more interesting bits in RKER are given below:

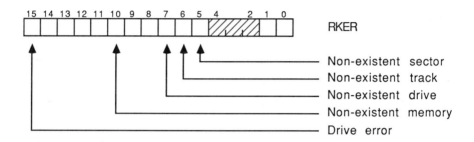

It can be seen from this that the error may be due to some fault in the parameters sent to the controller or to some fault with the drive. It is this distinction of error conditions that accounts, in part, for the two separate error indicators in RKCS. In the case of drive associated faults, further information as to the cause of the error may be extracted from the *drive status* register (RKDS), shown below:

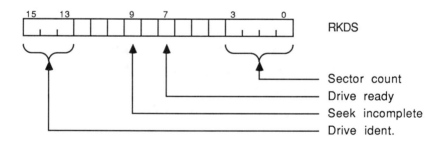

The bits in RKDS reflect the state of the drive identified by the program through bits 15 - 13 of the register.

8.5 Summary - Program/Controller Interaction

Direct Memory Access is used when it is impossible or undesirable for the program to organise its own transfers to or from the device. The device controller offers an approximation to the program that would be used but implemented in hardware. This could be viewed as a subroutine to the program requesting the transfer. The program detects the completion of the transfer (normal completion or error termination) either by means of a programmed loop or by use of the interrupt system. It is worth considering at this stage how the hardware acts as a subroutine to the program. This situation is particularly apparent if the program awaits completion with a programmed loop. Figure 8.1 shows what happens. The program sets up the parameters defining the transfer

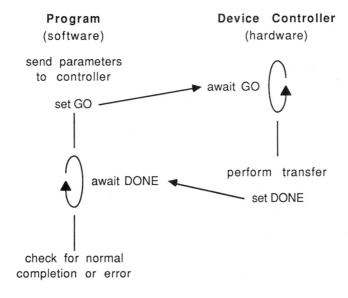

Figure 8.1 Interaction between software and hardware in DMA

and then tells the controller to GO. Up to this point, the controller has been waiting in what might be considered to be a programmed loop for the GO bit to be set. Upon completion of the transfer, the controller sets DONE which releases the program from its programmed loop wait and so on.

145

Chapter 9

Introduction to Operating Systems

9.1 The Rôle of the Operating System

It is the function of the operating system to provide the interface between users' programs running in the system and the hardware. In this context, especially when more than one user program is in the system at the same time, it is the job of the operating system to organise the *sharing* of system resources. These resources include the processor, the memory and the peripheral devices. In order that one user program running in the system does not interfere with others, the operating system must also organise *protection* of one user's share of the resources from the activities of all the other users.

The operating system is itself simply a program, although it is one with certain special characteristics.

In most situations in modern computer systems, it is desirable to allow more than one user to have access to the computer system at one time. These users may present their work to the system and then leave it to be processed *in due course* whilst others may sit at a terminal and interact directly with the system. This characteristic distinguishes between two major types of computer system. The former is some form of *batch* processing system whilst the latter represents a *multi-access* or *time-sharing* system. Although the detail of the operation of each of these systems differs, many of the features are the same. It is beyond the scope of this text to highlight all of the differences between these types of system.

In most computer systems, the operating system is responsible for providing a structure within which users may store programs and data in an organised fashion on a long term basis. This facility is provided by the *filing system* which divides up space on a backing store device such as a disk and shares it out amongst the users. In this case we see another need for the operating system to provide protection. Each user will expect his files to be safe from interference from other users.

9.1.1 Sharing of Resources

In any system that offers a service to a number of users on the same hardware, the operating system is responsible for organising the sharing of the resources. These resources include the processor, the memory and the peripherals. In order to give an idea of how the operating system contributes to the running of the complete computer system, the following sections outline how the operating system deals with the sharing of each of these resources.

9.1.1.1 Sharing the Processor

When the operating system has a number of user programs that are competing for processor time it will attempt to share out the time in such a way as to be as fair as possible to the programs without incurring major overheads. These overheads might be caused by the amount of processor time that the operating system itself requires to make decisions about which program to run next or they might be caused by incorrect or inappropriate decisions being made. In order to achieve its aim, the operating system usually places the programs into some sort of order and then shares out the time in *slots*. The order of the programs is determined by some pre-defined algorithm that takes account of a number of factors. These factors might include such thing as who owns the program or who has submitted it, how big it is in terms of memory requirement or what it has been doing over recent history. This latter factor is the most important in time-sharing systems. Once a program has had the processor assigned to it, the operating system may need to revoke this assignment at some time in the future. This decision to revoke the assignment is also influenced by one or more factors, some of which may be the same as those upon which the decision was made to run the program in question.

The program may be allowed to *run to completion*, but this is unlikely. The operating system will be more likely to restrict the amount of time that it is to allow the current program to have before giving the processor to another program. This amount of time might be fixed for all programs or might be some function of the program's past performance. In addition, the operating system is likely to remove the processor from the current program if it cannot continue to use the processor for some reason - for example, if it requires some input or output to take place.

It is clear that the processor is not given to one program until it completes and then to another and so on. Instead, the operating system gives the processor to one program for a while (the actual time defined by some aspect of operating system operation) and then passes it on to another for a while and so on.

It is the *processor scheduler* (or simply *scheduler*) that looks after the allocation of processor time to user programs.

9.1.1.2 Sharing the Memory

When the computer system is capable of supporting a number of user programs *at the same time*, it is clear that the programs must be stored in the same memory. The main problem to be solved here is how to arrange the programs within the memory such that the amount of memory wasted for one reason or another is minimised. There are many techniques available to solve this problem ranging from simply splitting up the memory into areas of similar size and placing one program in each through to much more complex techniques that allow parts of the program (and not necessarily all of it) to be placed into disjoint sections of memory. The latter is the result of the application of *segmentation* and/or *paging*. These two techniques were mentioned in passing in section 4.5 and rely upon extra hardware that is placed between the processor and the memory. This hardware will, in these techniques, be responsible for *mapping* addresses produced by the program (*virtual* addresses) into those that relate to the real memory (*real* addresses).

The *memory manager* is the part of the operating system that is responsible for sharing the memory amonst the user programs and its function is, quite reasonably, known as *memory management*.

9.1.1.3 Sharing Peripheral Devices

Some peripheral devices are inherently *shareable* whilst others are not. A disk system, for example, is ideally suited for use by a number of users. In general, the filing system will organise the allocation of space on the disk and will control access to the parts of the disk that are allocated to particular users. A request for the transfer of part of a file for one user might be followed by a similar request from another user. This second request can be satisfied before another request from the first user or another user comes along and so on.

On the other hand, a device like a printer would seem not to be shareable. Indeed it is not shareable at the same level as a disk system. We have seen how requests from two users for disk transfers might be *interleaved*. This cannot be allowed to happen in the case of a printer otherwise we would end up with printing from a number of users "jumbled up" on a single page of output. This is obviously not satisfactory. A device like a printer can be shared, however, on a longer term basis. The printer would have to be *allocated* to a particular user for the duration of a program run and then passed on to another user once the first had finished with it. Alternatively, the printer would not be allocated to specific users at all. Instead, all program output destined for a printer would be collected up on a disk file and printed at a later time - usually well after the program has terminated. This technique is known as *spooling* and may be applied to input also. In the latter case, all of the input for a program is read from the input device at one time - ahead of the program starting its run - and placed on to a disk file. As the program calls for data, the data previously stored on the disk file is substituted. This technique of *input spooling* is a favourite of batch systems.

In either case, the operating system is responsible for sequencing requests for transfers to and from the peripheral devices being always mindful of the characteristics of the device with respect to its inherent shareability.

9.1.2 Protection

There is a need for stringent protection throughout the computer system. In general we must be assured that any action of one user - accidental or malicious - must not be allowed to cause damage to another user's running program or stored files. Likewise it must not be allowed to cause disruption to the action or substance of the operating system. We will consider protection under the same three "sharing" headings of processor, memory and peripherals.

9.1.2.1 Protection of the Processor

At first sight there may not be much to protect at the processor level. In fact, the protection that is required here is against a user program taking over the processor and preventing the operating system and thence other user programs from gaining access to processor time. It is very easy for a program to become stuck in an *infinite loop* in which it is executing the same instructions over and over again making no progress towards completion or any other point at which the operating system can take over and re-distribute the processor. Remember that there is only one processor and hence when a user program is running, the operating system is not! The requirement here is for some special hardware that will periodically cause entry to the operating system so that it can check on what is happening. A simple device that causes an interrupt at regular intervals is all that is required. Often such a device is linked to the frequency of the mains in some way - hence the common name of *line time clock*.

9.1.2.2 Protection of the Memory

The need for protection is much more obvious here. Unless positive steps are taken to avoid it, the corruption of one user's memory space by the action of another user's program is highly likely. It only needs the program to fault in one of a number of ways in order for it to write to memory addresses that it has no right to access. If this memory *belongs* to another user, the second user's memory space has been violated and either his data has been corrupted or has been read without authority.

Certain memory management techniques require a great deal of additional hardware and software effort in order to provide an effective protection scheme. The simple memory management technique of simply splitting up the memory into similar size areas is a case in point. It requires the operating system to keep track of the bounds of the area(s) allocated to a particular program and also requires some hardware to ensure that no memory access from that user program falls outside the given bounds. As the scheduler selects the next user program to run, information relating to its memory allocation is passed down by the memory manager part of the operating system to this memory bound checking hardware. Thereafter, each and every access to memory is checked until either the program is suspended by the operating system or it terminates naturally.

Whilst the operating system is running, it is desirable to allow access to the whole of the memory. This is required so that the operating system may place any program and/or data it likes into the memory allocated to a particular program in readiness for its execution. The memory bound checking must be turned off or in some other way defeated during this time.

9.1.2.3   Protection of Peripheral Devices

The major requirement here is to prevent user programs from having *direct* access to any peripheral device. If access were allowed, chaos would ensue as each program would have its own ideas as to when and how to use each device that it requires. Instead, all input and output is performed by the operating system upon request from the user programs. User programs are prevented from gaining direct access by one of a number of mechanisms depending to some extent on how the devices are interfaced.

As was discussed in chapter 5, peripheral devices are accessed either as locations in memory (memory-mapped input/output) or by the use of special input and output instructions (port input/output). By imposing the memory bound checking mentioned in the previous section, any user program can be prevented from accessing any device connected in a memory-mapped fashion. Devices connected as port input/output devices pose another problem but this has almost as simple a solution. By restricting the user program's access to the instruction set, it is possible to prevent access to devices connected in this manner. Imposing this restriction, of course, requires an addition to the hardware of the processor. Any instruction set restrictions in operation for user program execution must be lifted whilst the operating system is running.

9.2 Hardware Assistance for the Operating System

Although the preceding sections have formed only an introduction to the rôle and function of an operating system, the indication is that the operating system requires some measure of assistance from hardware in order for it to function effectively. In fact, much of the hardware of the processor is provided with the operating system in mind. Most of the additional hardware functions are directed at protection and it is clear that there is a need to distinguish between the execution of user programs and the operating system. We now investigate how this is achieved.

9.2.1 Distinguishing Between the Operating System and Users

In almost every operating system situation, any hardware that is used to assist the operating system *must* be aware of whether the processor is running user program instructions or the operating system. For example, in memory management the mapping of virtual addresses to real addresses and the subsequently applied protection must be *enabled* whilst the processor is running the user program but will probably need to be *disabled* when the operating system takes over again. This is so that the operating system can have access to all of memory - via real addresses. In the case of peripheral protection, the processor must know whether to trap an attempt to execute an input/output instruction because it is the user program that is running or to allow it because the operating system is running.

Both of these cases (and many more) call for the processor to be capable of detecting whether it is running user program or is executing the operating system and to pass this information on to other parts of the hardware.

9.2.1.1 Two-State Processors

A *two-state* processor is one which runs in either one of two states. These two states denote that either:

(i) it is user code that the processor is running

or (ii) it is operating system code that the processor is running.

These two states are known by various names including:

(i)	(ii)
user state	special state
user mode	supervisor mode
normal mode	privileged mode

A flip-flop (the *state flip-flop*) within the processor is all that is needed to denote the current processor state. But under what conditions is the flip-flop set and cleared to denote the current state?

The transition from *User State* to *Special State* is made whenever the operating system is entered. Since the operating system is entered *only* on an interrupt, we can easily see that *any* interrupt should cause the flip-flop to denote special state. Note that as far as the operating system is concerned there are two distinct groups of interrupts. *System interrupts* come from devices within the system and say essentially "look at me" or "yes, I've done that, what now?". These are the interrupts that we have already seen in chapter 7 and are not *directly* associated with the running of the program - they are asynchronous. *Program (or process) interrupts* occur as a result of the execution of the current program instruction and are caused by, for example, an attempt to execute an illegal instruction or an attempt to access a memory location not assigned to the program. These are sometimes called *traps*.

The transition from *Special State* to *User State* must not take place until the operating system is finally ready to run a selected user program. Since it is the operating system's decision to return to running a user program and the operating system is in full control, it would seem obvious to let the operating system switch the flip-flop to user state. This it does by means of an instruction - effectively *switch to user state*. In order that the operating system may not then fall foul of any restrictions placed on program execution in user mode - for example, restricted instruction set or restricted access to memory - this instruction may be defined to not take effect until after the execution of the instruction following it. Thus the operating system sequence:

"switch to user state"
"return to user program"

would result in user state being established immediately prior to the execution of the first instruction of user code. This type of operation is comparable with that of the EI instruction on the Z-80.

9.2.1.2   Three-State Processors

When an interrupt occurs, then, the operating system is entered. The operating system immediately performs some tasks that are either time-critical or cannot be allowed to be interruped for some other reason. At some point later on, the operating system may be in a position to allow further interrupts even though it has not completed the servicing of the current one. It might therefore wish to enable interrupts again. In order to avoid this disabling and re-enabling of interrupts in a single special state, some processors have *three* states. The state entered on interrupt is a *non-interruptable special state* or *kernel state*. At a later time, the operating system can, by means of the execution of a given instruction "drop back" into an *interruptable special state* or *supervisor state*. Each of these two states are special states in the previously established context and as such have full access to both the instruction set and the memory. The only difference between kernel state and supervisor state is that in the former state interrupts are disabled and in the latter state they are enabled. These two states are, of course, in addition to the normal user state.

9.3 Operating System Structure

The modern operating system is typically made up of a number of distinct, independent procedures or *system processes*. Each of these has its own very specialised function to perform, for example looking after the filing system, running a peripheral device or scheduling user programs. Each of these processes is invoked as a result of an interrupt. The interrupt responsible might be a system interrupt or a program interrupt and the process might be invoked directly as a result of the interrupt or indirectly as part of the handling of the interrupt. In any case, processes will probably need to communicate with one another and will certainly have to be properly sequenced through their operations with respect to one another.

It is the job of the *kernel* of the operating system to receive an interrupt from the hardware and to decide which process should be responsible, in the first instance, for handling it. It will then inform the selected process that there is an interrupt for it to service. This process will often need the assistance of another process. The process requiring assistance will formulate a request and will need to pass it to the one which it has identified to provide the service. The actual passing of this request or *message* is carried out by the kernel. Once the message is received, the receiving process will probably have to run before the requesting process is able to continue. This sequencing is also administered by the kernel. The kernel is thus a scheduler of system processes which offers a message delivery service also.

The kernel must not be able to be interrupted as it has important decisions to make that affect the operation of the whole system and some of these decisions are likely to be time-critical. The system processes, on the other hand, are probably quite capable of being interrupted. It is therefore likely that the kernel will run in kernel (non-interruptable special) state on a three state machine and that the system processes will run in supervisor (interruptable special) state. This, of course, is the justification for three-state processors.

Figure 9.1 shows the typical organisation of an operating system based upon the principles outlined above.

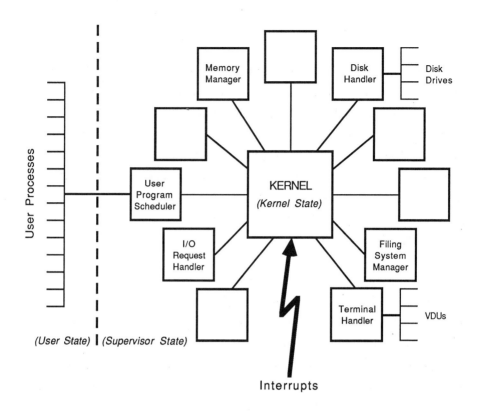

Figure 9.1 Operating System Organisation

Appendix A

Z-80 Pin Configuration, Organisation, and Timing

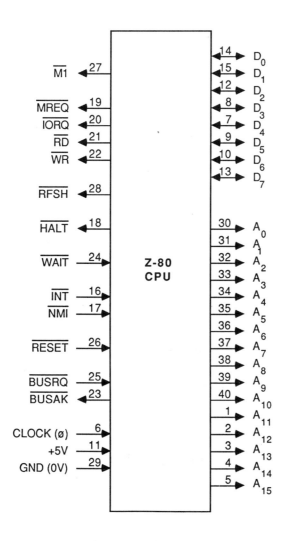

Z-80 Pin Configuration

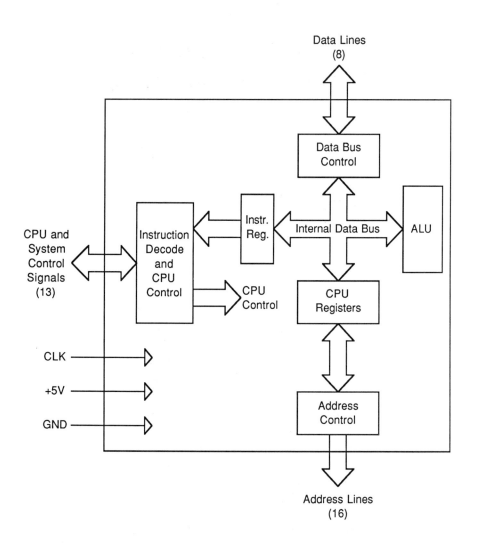

Z-80 Organisation

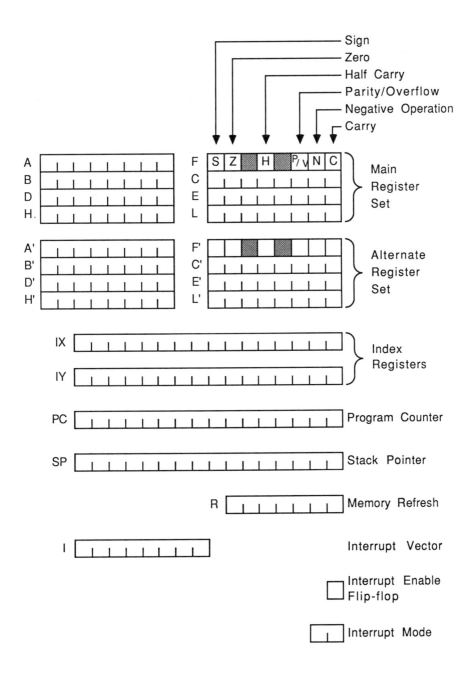

Z-80 Register Set

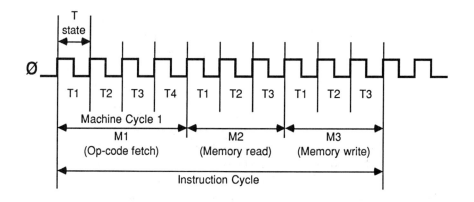

Z-80 Basic Timing

Appendix B

Z-80 Instruction Set

Mnemonic		Operation	S	Z	P/V	C
LD	r,s	r←s	-	-	-	-
LD	s,r	s←r	-	-	-	-
LD	s,n	s←n	-	-	-	-
LD	A,s	A←s	-	-	-	-
LD	s,A	s←A	-	-	-	-
LD	ss,nn	ss←nn	-	-	-	-
LD	ss,(nn)	ss←(nn)	-	-	-	-
LD	(nn),ss	(nn)←ss	-	-	-	-
LD	SP,nn	SP←nn	-	-	-	-
PUSH	ss	SP--; top of stack←ss	-	-	-	-
POP	ss	ss←top of stack; SP++	-	-	-	-
LDI		(DE)←(HL); DE++; HL++; BC--	-	x	x	↕
LDIR		repeat {(DE)←(HL); DE++; HL++; BC--} until BC=0	-	x	x	0
LDD		(DE)←(HL); DE--; HL--; BC--	-	x	x	↕
LDDR		repeat {(DE)←(HL); DE--; HL--; BC--} until BC=0	-	x	x	↕
INC	s	s←s+1	-	↕	↕	↕
DEC	s	s←s-1	-	↕	↕	↕
CPL		A←~A	-	-	-	-
NEG		A←-A	↕	↕	↕	↕
ADD	s	A←A+s	↕	↕	↕	↕
ADC	s	A←A+s+CY	↕	↕	↕	↕
SUB	s	A←A-s	↕	↕	↕	↕
SBC	s	A←A-s-CY	↕	↕	↕	↕
DAA		correct A to BCD after addition or subtraction	↕	↕	↕	↕
AND	s	A←A AND s	0	↕	↕	↕
XOR	s	A←A exclusive-OR s	0	↕	↕	↕

Instruction	Operand	Description				
OR	s	A←A OR s	0	↕	↕	↕
BIT	b,s	set Z flag to reflect state of bth bit of s	-	↕	x	x
CP	s	A-s (note result not stored, only flags set)	↕	↕	↕	↕
CPI		A-(HL); HL++; BC--	-	↕	x	↕
CPIR		repeat {A-(HL); HL++; BC--} until A=(HL) or BC=0	-	↕	x	↕
CPD		A-(HL); HL--; BC--	-	↕	x	↕
CPDR		repeat {A-(HL); HL--; BC--} until A=(HL) or BC=0	-	↕	x	↕
IN	A,(n)	A←port n [$<A_{15} - A_8> \leftarrow A$]	-	-	-	-
IN	r,(C)	r←port (C) [$<A_{15} - A_8> \leftarrow B$]	-	↕	↕	↕
OUT	(n),A	port n←A [$<A_{15} - A_8> \leftarrow A$]	-	-	-	-
OUT	(C),r	port (C)←r [$<A_{15} - A_8> \leftarrow B$]	-	-	-	-
INI		(HL)←port (C); HL++; B-- [$<A_{15} - A_8> \leftarrow B$]	-	↕	x	x
INIR		repeat {(HL)←port (C); HL++; B--} until B=0 [$<A_{15} - A_8> \leftarrow B$]	-	1	x	x
IND		(HL)←port (C); HL--; B-- [$<A_{15} - A_8> \leftarrow B$]	-	↕	x	x
INDR		repeat {(HL)←port (C); HL--; B--} until B=0 [$<A_{15} - A_8> \leftarrow B$]	-	1	x	x
OUTI		port (C)←(HL); HL++; B-- [$<A_{15} - A_8> \leftarrow B$]	-	↕	x	x
OTIR		repeat {port (C)←(HL); HL++; B--} until B=0 [$<A_{15} - A_8> \leftarrow B$]	-	1	x	x
OUTD		port (C)←(HL); HL--; B-- [$<A_{15} - A_8> \leftarrow B$]	-	↕	x	x
OTDR		repeat {port (C)←(HL); HL--; B--} until B=0 [$<A_{15} - A_8> \leftarrow B$]	-	1	x	x
EX	DE,HL	DE↔HL	-	-	-	-
EX	AF,AF'	AF↔AF'	-	-	-	-
EXX		BC↔BC'; DE↔DE'; HL↔HL'	-	-	-	-
EX	(SP),ss	top of stack←ss	-	-	-	-
INC	ss	ss←ss+1	-	-	-	-
DEC	ss	ss←ss-1	-	-	-	-
ADD	HL,ss	HL←HL+ss	↕	-	-	-
ADD	IX,ss	IX←IX+ss	↕	-	-	-
ADD	IY,ss	IY←IY+ss	↕	-	-	-
ADC	HL,ss	HL←HL+ss+CY	↕	↕	↕	↕
SBC	HL,ss	HL←HL-s-CY	↕	↕	↕	↕
SCF		CY←1	1	-	-	-
CCF		CY←~CY	↕	-	-	-

SET	b,s	set b[th] bit of s	- - - -
RES	b,s	reset (clear) b[th] bit of s	- - - -

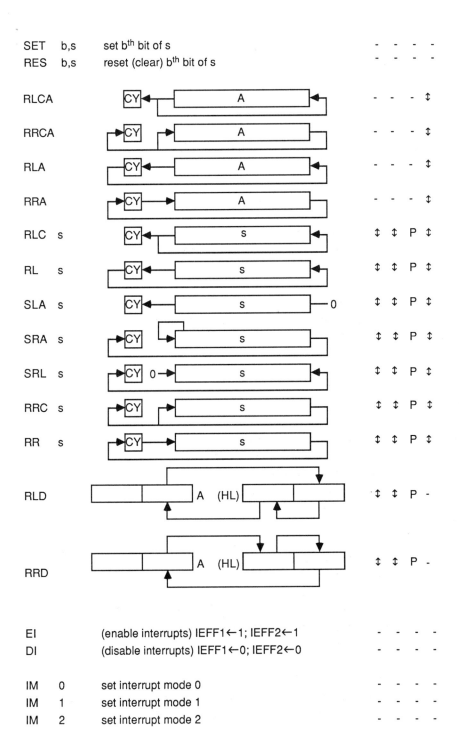

RLCA		- - - ↕
RRCA		- - - ↕
RLA		- - - ↕
RRA		- - - ↕
RLC s		↕ ↕ P ↕
RL s		↕ ↕ P ↕
SLA s		↕ ↕ P ↕
SRA s		↕ ↕ P ↕
SRL s		↕ ↕ P ↕
RRC s		↕ ↕ P ↕
RR s		↕ ↕ P ↕
RLD	A (HL)	↕ ↕ P -
RRD	A (HL)	↕ ↕ P -

EI		(enable interrupts) IEFF1←1; IEFF2←1	- - - -
DI		(disable interrupts) IEFF1←0; IEFF2←0	- - - -
IM	0	set interrupt mode 0	- - - -
IM	1	set interrupt mode 1	- - - -
IM	2	set interrupt mode 2	- - - -

HALT		set halt and wait for interrupt	-	-	-	-
NOP		no operation	-	-	-	-
JP	nn	jump unconditionally to nn (no limit)	-	-	-	-
JR	e	jump unconditionally relative by e	-	-	-	-
JP	cc,nn	jump on condition cc (cc=C, NC, Z, NZ, M, P, PE, PO)	-	-	-	-
JR	cc,e	jump relative on condition cc (cc=C, NC, Z, NZ)	-	-	-	-
JP	(HL)	jump indirect through HL	-	-	-	-
JP	(ss)	jump indirect through ss (ss=IX or IY)	-	-	-	-
DJNZ e		B--; jump relative by e if B=0	-	-	-	-
CALL nn		push PC; jump to nn	-	-	-	-
RST p		push PC; jump to p (p=0, 8, 10, 18, 20, 28, 30, 38 (hex))	-	-	-	-
CALL cc,nn		{push PC; jump to nn} if cc (cc as for JP)	-	-	-	-
RET		pop PC	-	-	-	-
RET cc		pop PC if cc (cc as for JP)	-	-	-	-
RETI		reset Z-80 family interface interrupt logic; pop PC	-	-	-	-
RETN		IEFF1←IEFF2; pop PC	-	-	-	-

Key

Operation: A←B means *B is copied to A*;
A↔B means *A and B are swapped*;
A++ means A is incremented;
A-- means A is decrementeded;
n is an 8-bit number;
nn is a 16-bit number;
d is an 8-bit signed numeric offset;
e is an 8-bit signed address offset;
r is an 8-bit register;
rr is a 16-bit register or register pair
s is an 8-bit operand usually from {r, (HL), (IX+d), (IY+d)};
ss is a 16-bit operand usually from {rr, (HL)};
CY is the carry flag

Flags: - means flag not affected; 0 means flag reset; 1 means flag set;
P means parity/overflow flag is used for parity;
↕ means flag affected to reflect result of instruction

Appendix C

6850 ACIA Pin Configuration and Organisation

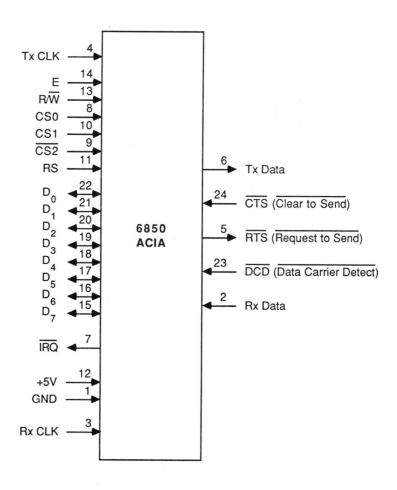

ACIA Pin Configuration

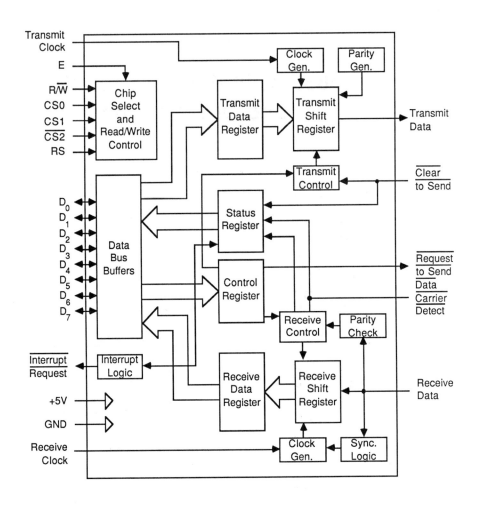

ACIA Organisation

	R/$\overline{\text{W}}$ = 0	R/$\overline{\text{W}}$ = 1
RS = 0	Control Register	Status Register
RS = 1	Transmit Data Register	Receive Data Register

ACIA Register Configuration

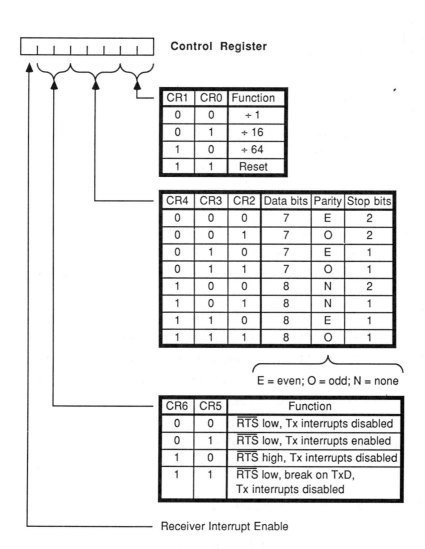

Control Register

CR1	CR0	Function
0	0	÷ 1
0	1	÷ 16
1	0	÷ 64
1	1	Reset

CR4	CR3	CR2	Data bits	Parity	Stop bits
0	0	0	7	E	2
0	0	1	7	O	2
0	1	0	7	E	1
0	1	1	7	O	1
1	0	0	8	N	2
1	0	1	8	N	1
1	1	0	8	E	1
1	1	1	8	O	1

E = even; O = odd; N = none

CR6	CR5	Function
0	0	RTS low, Tx interrupts disabled
0	1	RTS low, Tx interrupts enabled
1	0	RTS high, Tx interrupts disabled
1	1	RTS low, break on TxD, Tx interrupts disabled

Receiver Interrupt Enable

ACIA Control Register

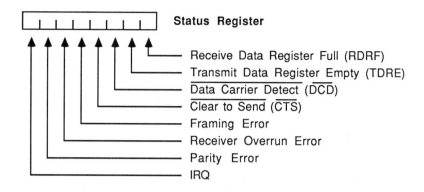

Status Register

- Receive Data Register Full (RDRF)
- Transmit Data Register Empty (TDRE)
- Data Carrier Detect ($\overline{\text{DCD}}$)
- Clear to Send ($\overline{\text{CTS}}$)
- Framing Error
- Receiver Overrun Error
- Parity Error
- IRQ

RDRF a 1 in this bit indicates that there is a character in the receive data register awaiting collection

TDRE a 1 in this bit indicates that the transmitter is in a position to be able to send any character placed into the transmit data register

$\overline{\text{DCD}}$ a 0 in this bit indicates that the data carrier is present (modem line)

$\overline{\text{CTS}}$ this bit reflects the state of the $\overline{\text{CTS}}$ input (modem line)

FE a 1 in this bit indicates the absence of the first stop bit resulting from character synchronisation error or faulty transmission (may be caused by incorrect Baud rate) or a *break* (open receiver) condition

OVRN a 1 in this bit indicates that at least one character was received but not collected from the receive data register

PE a 1 in this bit indiactes a failed parity check on the most recently received character

IRQ this is the complement of the $\overline{\text{IRQ}}$ output of the ACIA

ACIA Status Register

Appendix D

6850 ACIA Interrupt Program

The following is the assembly listing of a program to handle 6850 ACIA input and output by means of interrupts. This is intended to draw together a number of aspects of this text. In addition to demonstrating the principles of input/output programming by interrupts, it also demonstrates the principles of circular buffering. Necessarily, the program introduces the concept of a *critical section* of code whose execution must be guaranteed without interruption. Adequate notes on this and the other areas of interest are included in the comments which accompany the program.

The general form of each line of the source program is:

<label>: *<op-code>* *<destination-operand>*,*<source-operand>* ;*<comment>*

where the operands required depend upon the instruction op-code in use.

The general form of the assembly listing is:

address   assembled code   source line

where the assembled code might be 1, 2, 3 or 4 words long showing the op-code and the operand(s).

;PROGRAM TO RECEIVE CHARACTERS FROM THE ACIA BY INTERRUPTS AND TO
;ECHO AND BUFFER THEM. WHEN A CARRIAGE RETURN IS ENCOUNTERED, THE
;ENTIRE BUFFER FULL (WITH AN ADDED LINE-FEED ECHOED AND BUFFERED)
;IS OUTPUT TO THE SCREEN. DURING THIS PROCESS, ANY CHARACTERS
; TYPED BY THE USER ARE STILL ACCEPTED.

```
                ;DEVICE ADDRESSES

FF02            ACIACS   EQU  0FF02H      ;ACIA COMMAND AND STATUS REGISTERS
FF03            ACIADA   EQU  0FF03H      ;ACIA DATA REGISTERS


                ;INTERRUPT VECTOR SPACE DEFINITION

0003            VSPACE   EQU  3           ;VECTOR SPACE AT 300H


                ;INTERRUPT VECTOR ASSIGNMENTS

0002            ACIAIV   EQU  2           ;ACIA INTERRUPT RESPONSE (LS 8 BITS ONLY)


                ;ACIA MODE CONTROL WORD

0011            ACIAMD   EQU  11H         ;8 BITS + NO PARITY + 2 STOP BITS; /16 CLOCK


                ;BUFFER CONTROL

00FF            BUFMAX   EQU  255         ;MAX. BUFFER COUNT = BUFFER SIZE  (256) - 1
0400            BUFFER   EQU  400H        ;START OF CIRCULAR BUFFER (MUST BE
                                          ;ON *256 BOUNDARY)


                ;CHARACTER CONSTANTS

000D            CR       EQU  0DH         ;CARRIAGE RETURN
000A            LF       EQU  0AH         ;LINE FEED
```

;MAIN PROGRAM

0100	F3	START:	DI		;IN CASE THEY'RE ENABLED ON RE-ENTRY!
0101	31 0100		LD	SP,START	;INITIALISE STACK POINTER
0104	ED 5E		IM	2	;SELECT INTERRUPT MODE
0106	3E 03		LD	A,VSPACE	;POINT TO VECTOR SPACE
0108	ED 47		LD	I,A	;AND LOAD INTO INTERRUPT REGISTER
010A	3E 11		LD	A,ACIAMD	;PICK UP STANDARD ACIA MODE BITS
010C	F6 80		OR	80H	;SET RECEIVE INTERRUPT ENABLE
010E	32 FF02		LD	(ACIACS),A	;SEND IT TO ACIA
0111	32 0206		LD	(ACIACM),A	;AND SAVE IT AS CURRENT MODE
0114	26 03		LD	H,VSPACE	;PICK UP MS
0116	2E 02		LD	L,ACIAIV	;AND LS HALVES OF ACIA VECTOR ADDRESS
0118	11 0151		LD	DE,ISRACI	;SET UP
011B	73		LD	(HL),E	;AND PLANT ISR ADDRESS (LS AND
011C	23		INC	HL	;(BUMP POINTER)
011D	72		LD	(HL),D	;MS HALVES SEPARATELY)
011E	21 0400		LD	HL,BUFFER	;POINT TO START OF CIRCULAR BUFFER
0121	22 0201		LD	(FILPTR),HL	;AND USE THIS TO SET UP FILL
0124	22 0203		LD	(EMPPTR),HL	;AND EMPTY POINTERS TO BUFFER
0127	AF		XOR	A	;CLEAR A
0128	32 0205		LD	(BUFCNT),A	;AND USE THIS TO INITIALISE BUFFER COUNT
012B	32 0207		LD	(EOLN),A	;AND END OF LINE FLAG
012E	21 020A		LD	HL,INBUFF	;POINT TO START OF INPUT BUFFER
0131	22 0208		LD	(INPTR),HL	;AND USE IT TO PRESET INPUT BUFFER POINTER
0134	FB		EI		;ENABLE INTERRUPTS IN THE SYSTEM
0135	3A 0207	WAIT:	LD	A,(EOLN)	;PICK UP END OF LINE FLAG
0138	A7		AND	A	;LOOK AT IT
0139	CA 0135		JP	Z,WAIT	;NOT SET - GO LOOK AGAIN
013C	CD 01E9		CALL	COPY	;GOT A LINE - COPY IT ACROSS
013F	AF		XOR	A	;CLEAR A
0140	32 0207		LD	(EOLN),A	;AND USE IT TO SET END OF LINE FLAG
0143	3A 0206		LD	A,(ACIACM)	;PICK UP CURRENT ACIA MODE
0146	F6 20		OR	20H	;SET TRANSMIT INTERRUPT ENABLE
0148	32 FF02		LD	(ACIACS),A	;THEN SEND IT TO ACIA
014B	32 FF02		LD	(ACIACS),A	;AND SAVE IT AS CURRENT MODE
014E	C3 0135		JP	WAIT	;THEN GO WAIT AGAIN

```
                  ;INTERRUPT SERVICE ROUTINES

                  ;FOR ACIA.  FIRST, WE MUST LOOK AT THE ACIA STATUS TO FIND OUT IF IT'S
                  ;AN INPUT OR AN OUTPUT INTERRUPT.  WE DO THIS BY LOOKING AT THE
                  ;RECEIVER BIT (BIT 0 - RDRF).  IF THIS IS SET, WE ASSUME THAT IT IS A
                  ;RECEIVER INTERRUPT, OTHERWISE WE ASSUME THAT IT IS A TRANSMITTER
                  ;INTERRUPT.  WE THEN PROCEED AS FOLLOWS:
                  ;
                  ;         INPUT - TAKE CHARACTER AND ECHO OT BY PLACING IT IN THE
                  ;                 OUTPUT CIRCULAR BUFFER, THEN PLACE IT INTO THE
                  ;                 INPUT (LINEAR) BUFFER.  ENABLE TRANSMIT INTERRUPTS.
                  ;
                  ;     OUTPUT - ATTEMPT TO TAKE A CHARACTER FROM THE CIRCULAR
                  ;                 OUTPUT BUFFER.  IF THERE IS ONE, THEN OUTPUT IT,
                  ;                 ELSE CLEAR THE TRANSMIT INTERRUPT ENABLE.
                  ;
                  ;SINCE THE INTERRUPT SERVICE ROUTINES RUN WITH INTERRUPTS DISABLED,
                  ;WE DO NOT NEED TO WORRY ABOUT CALLING GETCHR AND PUTCHR WITH
                  ;RESPECT TO THEIR SHARED VARIABLES (SEE COMMENTS ON THE BUFFERING
                  ;ROUTINES PUTCHR AND GETCHR FOR DETAILS)

0151  F5        ISRACI:  PUSH AF          ;SAVE AF
0152  3A FF02            LD    A,(ACIACS)  ;PICK UP ACIA STATUS
0155  0F                 RRCA              ;LOOK AT RECEIVER BIT
0156  D2 018C            JP    NC,ISRXMT   ;NOT SET - MUST BE A TRANSMIT ONE
                                           ;'TIS SET - DROP INTO ...


                  ;RECEIVER INTERRUPT HANDLER

0159  E5                 PUSH HL           ;SAVE HL
015A  3A FF03            LD    A,(ACIADA)  ;PICK UP CHARACTER
015D  E6 7F              AND   7FH         ;STRIP PARITY BIT (MAINLY FOR COMPARISONS)
015F  2A 0208            LD    HL,(INPTR)  ;PICK UP CURRENT INPUT BUFFER POINTER
0162  77                 LD    (HL),A      ;BUFFER CHARACTER
0163  23                 INC   HL          ;BUMP BUFFER POINTER
0164  F5                 PUSH AF           ;SAVE CHARACTER
0165  CD 01A4            CALL  PUTCHR      ;PLACE CHARACTER IN OUTPUT BUFFER
                                           ;FOR ECHOING
0168  F1                 POP   AF          ;RESTORE CHARACTER
0169  FE 0D              CP    CR          ;WAS CHARACTER <CR>?
016B  C2 017D            JP    NZ,NOTCR    ;NO - SKIP
```

```
016E  3E 0A              LD    A,LF          ;YES - SET UP <LF>
0170  77                 LD    (HL),A        ;PLACE IT IN INPUT BUFFER
0171  23                 INC   HL            ;BUMP POINTER
0172  CD 01A4            CALL  PUTCHR        ;SEND <LF> TO OUTPUT BUFFER FOR ECHOING
0175  3E 01              LD    A,1           ;SET UP A 1
0177  32 0207            LD    (EOLN),A      ;AND USE IT TO SET END OF LINE FLAG
017A  21 020A            LD    HL,INBUFF     ;RESET POINTER TO TOP OF INPUT BUFFER
017D  22 0208    NOTCR:  LD    (INPTR),HL    ;RESTORE INPUT BUFFER POINTER
0180  3A 0206            LD    A,(ACIACM)    ;PICK UP CURRENT ACIA MODE
0183  F6 20              OR    20H           ;SET TRANSMIT INTERRUPT ENABLE BIT
0185  32 FF02            LD    (ACIACS),A    ;AND SEND IT TO ACIA
0188  E1                 POP   HL            ;RESTORE HL
0189  C3 01A1            JP    ISRRET        ;THEN RETURN


                        ;TRANSMITTER INTERRUPT HANDLER

018C  CD 01CB ISRXMT:  CALL GETCHR          ;PICK UP CHARACTER FROM OUTPUT BUFFER
018F  A7                AND   A             ;LOOK AT RETURNED CHARACTER
0190  CA 0199           JP    Z,NOOUT       ;NULL - THERE ARE NO CHARACTERS IN
                                            ;THE BUFFER
0193  32 FF03           LD    (ACIADA),A    ;THERE IS ONE - SEND IT
0196  C3 01A1           JP    ISRRET        ;THEN GET OUT


0199  3A 0206  NOOUT:  LD    A,(ACIACM)    ;PICK UP CURRENT ACIA MODE
019C  E6 DF             AND   0DFH          ;CLEAR TRANSMIT INTERRUPT ENABLE BIT
019E  32 FF02           LD    (ACIACS),A    ;AND SEND IT TO ACIA

                        ;GENERAL ISR EXIT

01A1  F1       ISRRET:  POP  AF             ;RESTORE AF
01A2  FB                EI                  ;RE-ENABLE INTERRUPTS
01A3  C9                RET                 ;THEN RETURN
```

;SUBROUTINES

;WE START WITH THE BUFFER HANDLING ROUTINES PUTCHR AND GETCHR.
;THESE ACCESS SHARED VARIABLES (BUFFER POINTERS AND COUNT), SO WE
;NEED SOME CODE TO PROTECT THIS "CRITICAL SECTION". IN MOST CASES
;THESE TWO ROUTINES ARE CALLED FROM INTERRUPT SERVICE ROUTINES
;AND SO WE DO NOT HAVE TO PROTECT THEM SPECIFICALLY. IN ONE CASE,
;WHEN WE COPY THE INPUT BUFFER TO THE OUTPUT BUFFER, THIS IS DONE AT
;THE MAIN PROGRAM LEVEL. IN ORDER TO AVOID POSSIBLE PROBLEMS WITH
;ACCESS TO THIS VARIABLE, THE COPY PROCESS IS PROTECTED BY
;DISABLING INTERRUPTS DURING BUFFERING. THIS WHOLESALE DISABLING OF
;INTERRUPTS COULD BE AVOIDED BY PROTECTING THE UPDATE OF THE
;SHARED VARIABLES EACH TIME THE UPDATE TAKES PLACE. THIS IS, OF
;COURSE, TIME CONSUMING.

;NOW THE ROUTINES ...

;PUTCHR - PLACES THE CHARACTER PASSED IN A INTO THE CIRCULAR
;BUFFER.
;THIS BUFFER IS DEFINED BY THREE ITEMS OF DATA:
;
;   FILPTR - BUFFER FILL POINTER. IT IS VIA THIS THAT DATA
;   IS PLACED INTO THE BUFFER.
;   EMPPTR - BUFFER EMPTY POINTER. IT IS VIA THIS THAT DATA
;   IS TAKEN OUT OF THE BUFFER.
;   BUFCNT - BUFFER COUNT. COUNTS THE NUMBER OF CHARACTERS
;   IN THE BUFFER.
;
;SINCE THE BUFFER LENGTH IS 256 AND THE BUFFER STARTS ON A MULTIPLE
;OF 256 ADDRESS BOUNDARY, THE BUFFER IS MADE CIRCULAR BY MAKING
;SURE THAT THE MOST SIGNIFICANT HALF OF THE ADDRESS DOES NOT
;CHANGE, BUT THAT THE LEAST SIGNIFICANT HALF SIMPLY COUNTS OVER AND
;OVER AGAIN.THIS IS DONE BY CHECKING THE LEAST SIGNIFICANT HALF OF
;THE ADDRESS EVERY TIME IS IT INCREMENTED FOR THE LEAST SIGNIFICANT
;HALF TO BE ZERO. IF IT IS, THE MOST SIGNIFICANT HALF IS DECREMENTED.
;
;PUTCHR RETURNS A ZERO (NULL CHARACTER) IN A IF THE CHARACTER WAS
;BUFFERED SUCCESSFULLY, ELSE IT RETURNS THE CHARACTER (ASSUMED
;TO BE NON-ZERO) IF THE BUFFER WAS FULL.

174

```
01A4 E5        PUTCHR: PUSH HL              ;SAVE HL
01A5 F5                PUSH AF              ;AND THE CHARACTER TO BE BUFFERED
01A6 3A 0205           LD   A,(BUFCNT)      ;PICK UP BUFFER COUNT
01A9 FE FF             CP   BUFMAX          ;IS THE BUFFER FULL?
01AB C2 01B1           JP   NZ,BSPACE       ;NO - THERE'S SPACE - GO BUFFER CHARACTER
01AE C3 01C8           JP   PUTFUL          ;YES - SKIP OUT WITH "ERROR" INDICATOR
01B1 3C        BSPACE: INC  A               ;COUNT CHARACTER INTO BUFFER
01B2 32 0205           LD   (BUFCNT),A      ;AND THEN SAVE COUNT IN MEMORY
01B5 F1                POP  AF              ;BRING BACK CHARACTER
01B6 2A 0201           LD   HL,(FILPTR)     ;PICK UP FILL POINTER
01B9 77                LD   (HL),A          ;BUFFER CHARACTER
01BA 23                INC  HL              ;BUMP POINTER
01BB 7D                LD   A,L             ;PICK UP LS HALF OF UPDATED POINTER
01BC A7                AND  A               ;LOOK AT IT
01BD C2 01C1           JP   NZ,PNTEND       ;IT'S NOT AT THE END OF THE BUFFER - SKIP
01C0 25                DEC  H               ;IT IS - RESET POINTER TO HEAD OF BUFFER
01C1 22 0201   PNTEND: LD   (FILPTR),HI     ;RESTORE FILL POINTER TO MEMORY
01C4 AF                XOR  A               ;CLEAR A FOR ...
01C5 C3 01C9           JP   PUTRET          ;NORMAL RETURN
01C8 F1        PUTFUL: POP  AF              ;BRING BACK CHARACTER (ERROR RETURN)
01C9 E1        PUTRET: POP  HL              ;RESTORE HL
01CA C9                RET                  ;THEN RETURN


;GETCHR - TAKES A CHARACTER FROM THE BUFFER AND RETURNS IT IN A.
;IF THERE IS NO CHARACTER, IT RETURNS A ZERO.


01CB 3A 0205   GETCHR: LD   A,(BUFCNT)      ;PICK UP BUFFER COUNT
01CE A7                AND  A               ;LOOK AT IT
01CF CA 01E8           JP   Z,GETRET        ;NOTHING THERE - RETURN WITH ZERO TO MARK
                                            ;NO CHARACTERS
01D2 3D                DEC  A               ;DISCOUNT CHARACTER
01D3 32 0205           LD   (BUFCNT),A      ;RESTORE COUNT
01D6 E5                PUSH HL              ;SAVE HL
01D7 2A 0203           LD   HL,(EMPPTR)     ;PICK UP EMPTY POINTER
01DA 7E                LD   A,(HL)          ;TAKE OUT CHARACTER
01DB 23                INC  HL              ;BUMP POINTER
01DC F5                PUSH AF              ;SAVE CHARACTER
01DD 7D                LD   A,L             ;PICK UP LS HALF OF UPDATED ADDRESS
01DE A7                AND  A               ;LOOK AT IT
01DF C2 01E3           JP   NZ,GNTEND       ;NOT AT THE END - SKIP
```

```
01E2  25              DEC   H            ;RESTORE POINTER TO START OF BUFFER
01E3  22 0203  GNTEND: LD   (EMPPTR),HL ;RESTORE POINTER TO MEMORY
01E6  F1              POP   AF           ;BRING BACK CHARACTER
01E7  E1              POP   HL           ;RESTORE HL
01E8  C9      GETRET: RET                ;THEN RETURN
```

;COPY - COPIES CONTENTS OF INPUT BUFFER (UP TO <LF>) TO THE
;CIRCULAR OUTPUT BUFFER. SINCE THIS ROUTINE IS ALWAYS CALLED FROM
;THE MAIN LOOP LEVEL WITH INTERRUPTS ENABLED, WE MUST PROTECT THE
;BUFFERING PROCESS BY DISABLING INTERRUPTS DURING THE CALL TO
;PUTCHR.

```
01E9  E5      COPY:   PUSH HL            ;SAVE HL
01EA  21 020A         LD   HL,INBUFF     ;POINT TO HEAD OF BUFFER
01ED  7E      COPYLP: LD   A,(HL)        ;PICK UP NEXT CHARACTER
01EE  23              INC  HL            ;BUMP POINTER
01EF  F5              PUSH AF            ;SAVE CHARACTER
01F0  F3      CPYTRY: DI                 ;PROTECT BUFFERING PROCESS (SEE NOTE
                                         ;ON SHARED VARIABLES)
01F1  CD 01A4         CALL PUTCHR        ;ATTEMPT TO PLACE CHARACTER IN
                                         ;OUTPUT BUFFER
01F4  FB              EI                 ;BUFFERING DONE - RE-ENABLE INTERRUPTS
01F5  A7              AND  A             ;LOOK AT RETURN
01F6  C2 01F0         JP   NZ,CPYTRY     ;NOT DONE IT DUE TO BUFFER FULL - TRY AGAIN
01F9  F1              POP  AF            ;BRING BACK CHARACTER
01FA  FE 0A           CP   LF            ;WAS IT LINE-FEED?
01FC  C2 01ED         JP   NZ,COPYLP     ;NO - MORE TO DO - LOOP
01FF  E1              POP  HL            ;RESTORE HL
0200  C9              RET                ;THEN RETURN
```

```
                    ;WORKSPACE

0201                FILPTR:  DS   2        ;CIRCULAR BUFFER FILL POINTER SAVE AREA
0203                EMPPTR:  DS   2        ;CIRCULAR BUFFER EMPTY POINTER SAVE AREA
0205  00            BUFCNT:  DB   0        ;BUFFER COUNT

0206  00            ACIACM:  DB   0        ;STORES CURRENT ACIA CONTROL WORD

0207  00            EOLN:    DB   0        ;END OF LINE FLAG

0208                INPTR:   DS   2        ;POINTER TO INPUT BUFFER



                    ;BUFFER SPACE


020A                INBUFF:  DS   128      ;RESERVE 128 CHARACTERS FOR INPUT BUFFER


                    END      START
```

Symbol table:

ACIACM	0206	ACIACS	FF02	ACIADA	FF03	ACIAIV	0002
ACIAMD	0011	BSPACE	01B1	BUFCNT	0205	BUFFER	0400
BUFMAX	00FF	COPY	01E9	COPYLP	01ED	CPYTRY	01F0
CR	000D	EMPPTR	0203	EOLN	0207	FILPTR	0201
GETCHR	01CB	GETRET	01E8	GNTEND	01E3	INBUFF	020A
INPTR	0208	ISRACI	0151	ISRRET	01A1	ISRXMT	018C
LF	000A	NOOUT	0199	NOTCR	017D	PNTEND	01C1
PUTCHR	01A4	PUTFUL	01C8	PUTRET	01C9	START	0100
VSPACE	0003	WAIT	0135				

No Fatal error(s)

Index